LEGENDS OF FLIGHT

MCDONNELL DOUGLAS DC-10/MD-11

A Legends of Flight Illustrated History

WOLFGANG BORGMANN

SCHIFFER MILITARY
4880 Lower Valley Road   Atglen, PA 19310

Originally published as *Die Flugzeugstars McDonnell Douglas DC-10* by Motorbuch Verlag, Stuttgart © 2019 Motorbuch Verlag
Translated from the German by David Johnston

Library of Congress Control Number: 2020943445

Cover design by Molly Shields
Type set in DIN/Minion Pro/Brandon Grotesque/Axia

ISBN: 978-0-7643-6137-1
Printed in China

Published by Schiffer Publishing, Ltd.
4880 Lower Valley Road
Atglen, PA 19310
Phone: (610) 593-1777; Fax: (610) 593-2002
E-mail: Info@schifferbooks.com
Web: www.schifferbooks.com

For our complete selection of fine books on this and related subjects, please visit our website at www.schifferbooks.com. You may also write for a free catalog.

Schiffer Publishing's titles are available at special discounts for bulk purchases for sales promotions or premiums. Special editions, including personalized covers, corporate imprints, and excerpts, can be created in large quantities for special needs. For more information, contact the publisher.

We are always looking for people to write books on new and related subjects. If you have an idea for a book, please contact us at proposals@schifferbooks.com.

CONTENTS

004   FOREWORD

014   **CHAPTER 1** ON THE WAY TO THE DC-10
THE DOUGLAS SAGA

030   **CHAPTER 2** ON THE WAY TO THE DC-10
FUSION OF THE GIANTS

036   **CHAPTER 3** ON THE WAY TO THE DC-10
THE FIRST WIDE-BODY JETS

046   **CHAPTER 4** ON THE WAY TO THE DC-10
TWO ARE ONE TOO MANY

050   **CHAPTER 5** MCDONNELL DOUGLAS DC-10
THE MOST SUCCESSFUL TRIJET

070   **CHAPTER 6** MCDONNELL DOUGLAS KC-10
THE FLYING FILLING STATION

074   **CHAPTER 7** MCDONNELL DOUGLAS DC-10
TANKER
IN USE AGAINST FOREST FIRES

078   **CHAPTER 8** MCDONNELL DOUGLAS MD-10
FROM FREIGHTER TO FLYING EYE HOSPITAL

084   **CHAPTER 9** ON THE WAY TO THE MD-11

087   **CHAPTER 10** MCDONNELL
DOUGLAS / BOEING MD-11
THE ULTIMATE TRIJET

102   **CHAPTER 11** THE DC-10 IN
THE LUFTHANSA GROUP
SELECTION BY THE ATLAS CONSORTIUM

112   **CHAPTER 12** DC-10 IN THE
LUFTHANSA GROUP
LOCKHEED TRISTAR WAS THE FAVORITE

116   **CHAPTER 13** MD-11 IN SERVICE
WITH THE LUFTHANSA GROUP
LUFTHANSA CARGO

124   **CHAPTER 14** LTU'S MD-11S
WORLD PREMIERE ABOVE THE CLOUDS

127   **CHAPTER 15** THE DC-10S OF
KLM, SAS, SWISSAIR, AND UTA
SELECTION BY THE KSSU CONSORTIUM

136   **CHAPTER 16** SPECIFICATIONS
DC-10/MD-11/MD-XX

FOREWORD

When I think back on the era of the McDonnell Douglas DC-10, it brings to mind wonderful memories of a great flight to North America. I will never forget the view of the Greenland ice shield from the large cabin windows of the SAS DC-10 Frode Viking, the approach to Anchorage over the Gompertz Channel onboard LN-RKA Olav Viking, the lights of Chicago after a night takeoff in Sverker Viking, and the shimmering green northern lights that accompanied Haakon Viking for hours during a flight from Seattle to Copenhagen on my way back to Europe. I will also never forget the uneasy feeling onboard American Airlines DC-10 N151AA while taking off from Chicago O'Hare—just a few years after the crash for which American took responsibility, which not only affected the airline's reputation but damaged that of the DC-10 and the McDonnell Douglas aircraft company as well. The disaster of Flight AA 191, which tragically resulted in the deaths of 273 people on May 25, 1979, is an ongoing reminder to the industry that in aviation, profit must never come before flight safety. In the hysteria that followed the accident, the DC-10's reputation suffered irreparable

United Air Lines and American Airlines were the first customers for the medium-range DC-10-10. Both airlines received their first jets during a handover ceremony at Long Beach on July 29, 1971. *Jon Proctor*

damage, which forced McDonnell Douglas to abandon the DC (Douglas Commercial) initials used since the DC-1 of 1933. The temporary grounding ordered by the FAA, the American regulatory agency, was neither the first nor the last grounding of an aircraft type as a result of safety concerns. But who still links the Lockheed Constellation, Douglas DC-6 Cloudmaster, or Lockheed L-188 Electra with their initial design flaws, as a result of which numerous persons lost their lives? And who thinks nowadays while flying on a Boeing 787 Dreamliner that this aircraft type was spared catastrophes only by good luck and that the FAA ordered all jets of this type grounded in 2013 until its defects were resolved.

If one considers the statistics concerning the aircraft types with the most accident fatalities, given the number of aircraft built, a flight in a DC-10 was surely safer than one in a Boeing 747 Classic or a Douglas DC-8. Like the DC-10, these air travel veterans are still used only as freighters. The last DC-10 used for passenger services was retired from service in February 2014 and scrapped soon afterward. Ironically, passenger use of its MD-11 successor also ended in November of that year—after the Dutch airline KLM retired its last example. And that was just twenty-four years after the type's first flight. For KLM the retirement of its last MD-11 was the emotional finale to an eighty-year story that began with the delivery of the first DC-2 propeller-driven airliner in 1934. This type was followed by the DC-3, DC-4, DC-5, DC-6, DC-7, DC-8, DC-9, and DC-10, up to the final MD-11.

DC-10 customers received promotional stickers like this one when their aircraft were delivered by McDonnell Douglas. *Author's archive*

The DC-10 currently remains in service around the globe, not in passenger service but on humanitarian missions. The trijet donated to Orbis by the express freight organization FedEx in 2011 was turned into a flying eye hospital with operating room, laser treatment center, and training areas for instructing and mentoring local doctors. The MD-10 and its team of volunteer doctors travel primarily to destinations in Asia, Africa, and Latin America, where the availability of local eye specialists is the worst and the need is therefore the greatest. The MD-10, which took to the air in 2010 after a lengthy conversion process, is the third jet—after a DC-8-21 and a DC-10-10—that Orbis has financed with charitable donations, and with which it operates a nongovernmental organization (NGO) for global treatment of people with eye problems.

Like all other Douglas aircraft types, the DC-10 is characterized by reliability and longevity. While the comparable Lockheed L-1011 TriStar has already been retired from service, and only a few Boeing 747-200s and -300s remain active with air freight companies, the DC-10, the KC-10, and the modernized MD-10 remain very popular. As this book was being written, 110 aircraft were still reported active, including fifty-nine KC-10s and thirty-eight MD-10s. Federal Express does not plan to finally retire the latter type until the year 2021. There are also 134 MD-11s, of which Federal Express, UPS Airlines, and Lufthansa Cargo maintain the largest fleets.

And so the friends of the last big trijet will have the opportunity to enjoy seeing these elegant machines at the world's airports for a few more years. I hope that you enjoy browsing through this richly illustrated book about the turbulent story of the DC-10 and MD-11.

Wolfgang Borgmann
Oerlinghausen, January 2019

The Scandinavian airline SAS, Swissair, and KLM introduced the DC-10-30 long-range version into service. SAS

This evocative image shows a Swissair DC-10-30 flying over the fog-filled valleys of the Swiss Alps. *ETH-Bibliothek Zurich, Swissair*

The German charter airline Condor used up to five DC-10-30s on its long-distance tourist routes for twenty years, from 1977 to 1997. *Condor*

Among the aircraft that LTU of Dusseldorf used to replace its popular L-1011s were three McDonnell Douglas MD-11 passenger jets. *LTU*

Test flight by a Swissair DC-10-30 prior to its delivery to the Swiss airline. *ETH-Bibliothek Zurich, Swissair*

SAS jetzt mit DC-10 nach Ost- und Südafrika.

Das bedeutet
für Sie:
Mehr
Frachtkapazität
durch
unseren Paletten-
und
Liftainer Service.

Fragen Sie
Ihren IATA Spediteur
oder Ihr nächstgelegenes
SAS Frachtbüro.

SAS CARGO
–the worldwide word for reliability.

SAS operated DC-10s from Copenhagen on its African routes. The aircraft made stops in Zurich, Vienna, and Athens during the flights to and from Dar-es-Salaam, Nairobi, and Johannesburg. *Author's archive*

Despite its size, the DC-10 was an extremely elegant airliner. *ETH-Bibliothek Zurich, Swissair*

CHAPTER 1
ON THE WAY
TO THE DC-10
THE DOUGLAS SAGA

THE DC-10 WAS THE TENTH AND LAST DESIGN IN THE LONG LINE OF DOUGLAS COMMERCIAL CIVIL AIRCRAFT THAT BEGAN WITH THE DC-1 IN 1933.

The initiator of the DC-1 was Jack Frye, president of Transcontinental and Western Airlines (TWA), whose order provided the foundation of an unequaled family of aircraft. After the prototype took off on its successful first flight on July 1, 1933, the DC-1 received its type certification just four months later. With its two Weight Cyclone radial engines, each producing 710 hp, it could carry twelve passengers—two more than its competitor, the Boeing 247. The DC-1 was also faster and had greater range than its archrival. Jack Frye was enthusiastic about the type's great potential and was also the first to order the larger DC-2, with its wider and longer fuselage.

The next evolutionary step for the DC family had its origins in a requirement issued by American Airlines president C. R. Smith. He planned to use an aircraft with fourteen bunk beds on nocturnal transcontinental routes across the United States. The fuselage of the DC-2 was therefore widened further, the cabin roof was raised, the wingspan was increased, and a new tail was designed. Initially called

A KLM MD-11 was turned into a light object on the occasion of the celebrations on October 7, 2014, marking the airline's ninety-fifth anniversary.

The metal skin of this Douglas DC-3 of the Flygande Veteraner, based in Stockholm, gleams in the Scandinavian sun.
Wolfgang Borgmann

the Douglas Sleeper Transport (DST), the DC-3 was born. The prototype flew for the first time on December 17, 1935, and with 455 civil examples and almost 20,000 military versions built, it became one of the most produced aircraft in the world—and remains in use in significant numbers to this day.

The first four-engined Douglas propeller-driven airliner went back to William A. "Pat" Patterson, president of United Air Lines, who approached Donald Douglas with an idea and 300,000 US dollars as enticement. Patterson was impressed by the twin-engined Douglas products, but he was looking for a manufacturer of an even-larger, four-engined commercial aircraft. Donald Douglas agreed to construction of the DC-4E Experimental, which could carry thirty passengers on night flights or forty-two passengers by day, with a degree of comfort that far surpassed that onboard the DST. A special feature of the DC-4E was its three-part tail, comparable

to that of the Lockheed Constellation. As promising as the performance figures of the DC-4E were, with war coming in Europe the airlines were reluctant to place orders. Douglas no doubt had a good aircraft, but one too large for a shrinking market. Even before the United States was drawn into the war, Donald Douglas decided to reduce the dimensions of a DC-4 production aircraft. He began setting up a final-assembly line in Santa Monica, California, for the production of twenty-four examples of the DC-4A for American Airlines and United Air Lines.

Douglas had less fortune with his DC-5, since only thirteen examples of this twin-engined shoulder-wing monoplane derived from the Douglas A-20 Boston/Havoc bomber left the final-assembly line at the Douglas factory in El Segundo. Douglas began construction of the prototype in September 1938, and the aircraft took to the air for the first time on February 12, 1939. Unlike the aircraft types

The liaison between Douglas and KLM from 1934 until 2014 began with the Douglas DC-2. *Author's archive*

The aircraft shown in the photo, a Lisunov L-2 built at Aircraft Factory 85 in 1949, is the license-built Soviet version of the American bestseller the Douglas DC-3. Both the USSR and Japan purchased rights to build the type under license before the outbreak of the Second World War. A team led by engineer Boris Lisunov studied Douglas's production techniques in the United States before production of the PS-84, later called the Li-2, began in the Soviet Union. In total, 6,157 aircraft were produced in the USSR before production ended in the mid-1950s. Russia also received more than 700 C-47s during the war, which were equipped with Russian AS-62 engines and designated TS-62. The Li-2, which was photographed on the ramp of the Hamburg airport in 2003, was delivered to the Hungarian military in 1949. It was subsequently operated by Malev Hungarian Airlines. *Author's archive*

The former German charter airline Aerotour operated DC-4s on its routes.
Author's archive

previously developed by Douglas, the DC-5 was not built at the request of a customer, but instead because it was technically possible to develop the A-20 into a commercial aircraft. With a seating capacity almost identical to that of the DC-3, the DC-5 offered no significant technical or operational improvements compared to its sister aircraft, and so the airlines had little incentive to procure the type. Ironically it was Boeing founder and owner William Edward Boeing who purchased the first DC-5, to be built as his personal aircraft. The first customer for the production aircraft was the US Navy, which procured three examples of the military version of the DC-5, the R3D-1, at the end of the year. Four more aircraft went to the Marine Corps as the R3D-2. The only airline customer for the type was KLM, which because of the outbreak of war in Europe transferred the aircraft to KNILM (Royal Dutch Indies Airways), based in the Dutch East Indies—present-day Indonesia.

With the DC-6 Cloudmaster, the Douglas Aircraft Co. succeeded in matching the civil success of its legendary DC-3 Dakota. While the military variants of its predecessor, the DC-4, were successful, after 1945 retired military aircraft swamped the market for used aircraft and made the sale of new DC-4s almost impossible. A commercial breakthrough with a successful type was therefore desperately needed, and Douglas undoubtedly achieved this, selling 175 examples of the DC-6 and 286 of the more powerful DC-6B.

The DC-6 resembled its predecessor—the DC-4—in many respects. A much-modified DC-4 (C-54) powered by Pratt & Whitney R-2800-22W engines, with the US Air Force designation YC-112, served as prototype for the civil DC-6 and its military sister the C-118. The YC-112 began its flight test program on February 15, 1946, this date serving as the official date of the first flight by the DC-6. From the beginning, the DC-6 was very popular with the

Douglas DC-4s also regularly visited the Stuttgart airport in the 1950s, including aircraft in Air France colors flying to Paris. *Flughafen Stuttgart GmbH*

airlines, mainly because of its pressurized cabin, which gave the Cloudmaster a much-higher cruising altitude than its predecessors. American Airlines and United Air Lines took charge of their first aircraft at Santa Monica, California, on March 28, 1947.

Joy over the new aircraft acquisitions was short lived, however, after a United Air Lines DC-6 crashed on fire at Bryce Canyon in Utah during a flight from Los Angeles to Chicago, while a second DC-6 flown by American Airlines caught fire over New Mexico on November 11, 1947. While the United accident ended in catastrophe, the American Airlines crew was able to make an emergency landing. Everyone onboard the aircraft managed to evacuate safely, and the flames were extinguished. Unlike with the first accident, investigators had the chance to thoroughly examine the aircraft and determine the cause. To avoid further accidents, as a precautionary measure all Douglas DC-6s that had been delivered were grounded on November 12, 1947. The accident investigators soon determined that fuel, which had leaked from the wing tanks due to a design error, had ignited in the cabin-heating equipment. Douglas worked to quickly put right the error, and on March 21, 1948, almost a year after the first deliveries, the DC-6s were back in the air. The accidents and subsequent grounding damaged neither the type's popularity nor Douglas's reputation. This is perhaps due in part to the fact that flying was then generally less safe, and therefore crashes were rather more common than they are today. Even while the DC-6 was grounded, Douglas worked on further developments of the type, with the designations DC-6A and DC-6B. Both variants had a stretched fuselage and greater range compared to the basic version. Unlike the DC-6B, however, the DC-6A was designed almost exclusively for carriage of freight. After their maiden flights, which took place on September 29, 1949 (DC-6A), and February 10, 1951 (DC-6B), the first freighters were delivered to Slick Airways, and the first passenger aircraft to United Air Lines.

The Douglas DC-7C was at the end of a long evolutionary chain of propeller-driven airliners from this manufacturer. Once again it was the president of American Airlines, C. R. Smith, who provided the impetus for development of the DC-7. He had previously convinced Douglas to build the DC-3 in 1934 and thus laid the cornerstone for the successful story of the aircraft manufacturer from Santa Monica. Now Smith requested a further development of the DC-6B, which Douglas delivered in the form of the DC-7, which first flew on May 18, 1953. An aircraft of this type first entered service with American Airlines on November 4, 1953, enabling nonstop flights between the American East and West Coasts.

Eastern Airlines initiated the DC-7B, which first flew on April 21, 1954, and had about 560 miles' greater range compared to the DC-7. It was followed by the ultimate DC-7C Seven Seas long-range version. Pan American was the first customer for this type, which entered service with the airline on April 18, 1956, mainly serving destinations on its wide-ranging network of routes in the Pacific. The DC-7C was thus available about a year earlier than its direct competitor, the Lockheed L-1649A Starliner. The DC-7C also served with many European airlines, including BOAC, KLM, Swissair, and SAS.

The radical change: Donald Douglas was at first hesitant to develop a long-range jet airliner, since the Douglas DC-7 was still selling well and its customers feared the loss of value of their Douglas prop-liners, which were only a few years old. But advances in

A Douglas DC-6 of Eagle Airways, a British airline established by Harold Bamberg in 1948. It was active both in scheduled and charter services and in 1968 was forced to declare bankruptcy. *Author's archive*

technology and the advantages of jet aviation could not be stopped. And so Douglas accepted the challenge from Boeing and developed a jetliner of comparable size and design to the Boeing 707. The DC-8A domestic version for continental routes within the United States was initially announced for 1956, while the DC-8B overwater variant for intercontinental routes was to become available in 1958.

Pan American president Juan T. Trippe began the orders dance on October 13, 1955, when he ordered up to twenty-five examples of the overwater version of the DC-8 with four Pratt & Whitney JT4 engines. At the same time he ordered just twenty Boeing 707-120s. The future looked especially rosy for Douglas after Trippe announced that in the future he wanted to order more DC-8s in place of Boeing 707s.

Just twelve days after Pan Am, United Air Lines placed an order for thirty DC-8s, followed by the Dutch airline KLM, the type's first overseas customer. By the end of 1955 the Douglas order books were filled with other orders from prominent customers such as Eastern Air Lines (26), National Airlines (6), Japan Air Lines (4), and Scandinavian Airlines (7).

Development of the DC-8 took longer than Douglas had originally planned. In June 1956, the company announced that it was setting up a new final-assembly line in Long Beach, California, especially for the DC-8. The first aircraft parts were completed in September 1956, and in addition to the production building, Douglas built a huge water tank that could accommodate a complete DC-8 fuselage for material fatigue tests. After the crash of the de Havilland Comet due to materials fatigue, Douglas fitted the DC-8 with small titanium crack arrestors on the fuselage frames and all cutouts, such as doors, service hatches, and windows. After 113,000 simulated flights in the water tank, a crack developed in an aluminum window frame; however, it was stopped by the arrestor, as planned, with a large margin of safety. The engineers simulated 120,000 flights with the cabin pressurized before the DC-8's first flight and ended the program with another 20,000 uneventful takeoffs and landings. The DC-8 had successfully proven its reliability. The prototype of the new Douglas design, Ship One, took to the air for the first time on May 30, 1958. After an extensive flight test program and certification by the FAA on August 31, 1959, the first customers—United Air Lines and Delta Air Lines—placed their newly delivered DC-8-11s into scheduled service simultaneously on September 18, 1959. This domestic version was followed by the DC-8-20, -30, -40, and -50. All these variants had the same fuselage length, but different power plants and ranges. The first major evolutionary step was the DC-8 Super Sixty models—DC-8-61, -62, and -63—with lengthened fuselages. Until the first flight of the Boeing 747 in December 1969, the DC-8-63, which was certified to carry 269 passengers, was the largest Western airliner.

The Series 62 and 63 also had Pratt & Whitney JT3D turbofan engines installed in slender engine pods. They also had aerodynamically improved wings and much-greater range—that of the DC-8-62 was approximately 10,000 kilometers (6,213 miles). After it became apparent, especially in the 1970s, that stronger noise regulations would take effect, especially in the United States, various North American airlines turned to Douglas with the request for quieter engine options for those DC-8s that had been in use for years. Pratt & Whitney offered its new JT8D-209 engine, while Cammacorp, which had been founded by retired Douglas managers, offered the significantly quieter and fuel-efficient CFM-56-1 to reengine the DC-8 versions -61, -62, and -63.

After United Air Lines and Flying Tiger Lines decided in favor of the Cammacorp concept, further contracts quickly followed, including from Delta Air Lines and Cargolux. In 1981, the FAA issued certifications for the DC-8-71, -72, and -73 models.

The DC-9, which competed with the Boeing 737, was a bestseller, especially in the 1970s, and helped McDonnell Douglas survive even in difficult times. After the crash of an American Airlines DC-10 in 1979, the favorable order situation allowed the company to stay above water.

The DC-9 prototype made its first flight on February 25, 1965, and this was followed by an intensive flight test program, before the first production version of the aircraft, the DC-9-14, entered service with Delta Air Lines on December 8, 1965. Within a few months, Continental, Eastern, and TWA also received their first aircraft, introducing jet comfort even on less frequented routes. As popular as this first version of the DC-9 was, the initial customers quickly parted with their DC-9-10s as soon as larger versions with lower operating costs became available.

The Dutch airline KLM was the first European airline to order the new jet from Long Beach, California. The DC-9-15 with the name City of Amsterdam was delivered on March 25, 1966, and it was followed by five more aircraft of the same type. Starting in November 1967, KLM expanded its fleet by thirteen larger DC-9-32s, while the Flying Dutchmen placed six DC-9-33RC Rapid Change variants in service in 1968–69. The aircraft had a side cargo door on the main deck and could be converted from a pure passenger version into a freighter in a short time.

In the mid-1960s, the manufacturer developed the DC-9-21 and DC-9-41, two versions tailor-made for the Scandinavian airline SAS, which since its creation in July 1946 had flown primarily Douglas designs. The first DC-9-41, with the name Heming Viking and the registration OY-KGA, arrived in Scandinavia on February 29, 1968, and one month later began scheduled services on the Copenhagen–Stockholm route. While the DC-9-41 served on SAS's European routes, the DC-9-21 was initially used on Norwegian domestic routes before it was also used on longer European routes. Swissair was the first customer for the last version marketed exclusively as the DC-9, before Douglas completed another major evolutionary step in the basic DC-9 design with the family of aircraft designated MD-80 and MD-90. Compared to the DC-9-10 basic model, the Series 51 had a fuselage lengthened by 29 feet and more-powerful Pratt & Whitney JT8D-17 engines. Altogether, twelve DC-9-41s were operated by Swissair from August 1975 onward. Other European customers for this type were Austrian Airlines, Itavia, and Finnair. Beginning in 1983, McDonnell Douglas marketed the DC-9-80 as the MD-80, ending the legendary Douglas Commercial series of aircraft.

DC-8 fuselage assembly in the Douglas Long Beach factory. SAS

We started the DC-10 36 years ago.

Our Douglas Aircraft Company has been building commercial airliners without interruption for 36 consecutive years. Now, there's a new DC Age coming—the era of the DC-10 family of luxury tri-jets. For air travelers, the DC-10 promises an environment of total comfort and convenience surpassing today's highest standards. For airlines, the DC-10 means a new level of versatility, reliability, and operating economy. Watch for the DC-10 in 1971. It's the new-generation jetliner from McDonnell Douglas, the people who have made DC a way of flight since 1933.

MCDONNELL DOUGLAS

1933 The 14-passenger DC-1 flew July 1, and the DC Age was born.

1934 The DC-2, 19 world speed records.

1935 Venerable DC-3 "workhorse" of the airlines.

1937 The DC-5, pre-empted by demand for 4-engined airliners.

1942 10,000 DC-3s go to war as the famed C-47 "Gooney Bird."

1946 DC-4s return from military to commercial duty.

1947 The DC-6, a new concept of comfort and spaciousness.

1953 Long range and 360 mph cruising speed won the DC-7 global acclaim.

1964 DC-9 twinjets brought jet service to smaller cities the world over.

1965 Super DC-8s are the largest, most advanced jetliners now in service.

This McDonnell Douglas Aircraft Company advertisement for the DC-10 shows the Douglas Commercial family of aircraft—beginning with the DC-1 from 1933. *Dave Robinson collection*

KLM was one of Douglas's most loyal customers for more than seven decades. The oldest airline in the world still flying under its original name, it purchased every civil aircraft type made by Douglas, from the DC-2 of 1934 to the DC-10-30. These included the unsuccessful DC-5, of which KLM bought four, making it the only airline in the world to fly the type. This long business relationship ended in 1990 with an order for ten examples of the McDonnell Douglas MD-11, developed from the DC-10. By that time, the Dutch airline had already severed its close ties with its traditional provider of aircraft and for the first time operated a direct competitor of a Douglas product, the Boeing 737-300. When it retired its last MD-11s in November 2014, KLM applied the special paint scheme seen here to one of the MD-11s still in its fleet. *KLM*

The fascinating panorama of the Swiss mountains was often chosen by Swissair as the background for press photos. This is also true of this photo of the MD-11 named Graubünden, with the registration HB-IWB, in flight over the western Bern Alps. *ETH-Bibliothek Zurich, Swissair*

CHAPTER 2
ON THE WAY
TO THE DC-10
FUSION OF THE GIANTS

Both Donald Wills Douglas Sr. and James Smith McDonnell Jr. had Irish roots, attended the renowned Massachusetts Institute of Technology (MIT) in Boston, and found their vocation and calling in the aviation industry. Donald Douglas Sr. was born in New York on April 6, 1892, and very early on discovered his interest in aviation, when after his studies, in 1915, while employed by Glenn Martin, he designed his first aircraft, and in 1920 he established his own aircraft company. Born in Denver on April 9, 1899, McDonnell Jr. officially made himself independent in 1926, and for several years he continued working on subcontracts for other companies before dedicating himself 100 percent to his own company in 1939.

While Douglas had success with the manufacture of civil passenger aircraft and military transports, from the beginning McDonnell focused on the production of combat jets. Located in St. Louis, the McDonnell Aircraft Company was just three months old when the Second World War broke out. After building tail sections and engine cowlings for the Douglas C-47 under license, on July 29, 1941, McDonnell received his first contract from the US

In terms of sales figures, the F-4 Phantom II, with 5,201 examples built at the McDonnell factory in St. Louis and by licensees, was second only to the DC-3 in the history of McDonnell Douglas. The F-4, which first flew on May 27, 1958, was the standard equipment of many Western air forces for decades. *NASA*

Formation flight by a McDonnell Douglas F-15B Advanced Control Technology for Integrated Vehicles (ACTIVE) and an F-18 escort aircraft. NASA began a program to investigate thrust vectoring on March 27, 1996, for which the NASA F-15 research aircraft was developed in cooperation with Pratt & Whitney. It was equipped with engine nozzles that could swivel 20 degrees in any direction. The research project revealed that thrust-supported flight control enabled significant improvements in flight characteristics both for military and civil aircraft programs in the subsonic and supersonic speed ranges. *NASA / Jim Ross*

Army Air Corps for a development of its own. The P-67 Bat was designed as a twin-engine interceptor fighter; however, it did not fly for the first time until January 6, 1944. After its flight characteristics left something to be desired, the US Army Air Force canceled construction of a second example. After the sole example was destroyed in a fire on September 6, 1944, the only piston-engined aircraft designed by McDonnell ended in dramatic fashion. The end of the P-67 did not, however, mean the end of the McDonnell Aircraft Company, which from 1942 was drawn into the development of the then-new jet technology. On January 7, 1943, McDonnell officially received a contract to develop the XFD-1, which on January 26, 1945, took to the air as the US Navy's first jet and was produced as the FH-1 Phantom. McDonnell then created the F2H Banshee and the F3H Demon before the company achieved its greatest success. After its maiden flight on May 27, 1958, the second jet with

the name Phantom became the F-4 Phantom II, which remains in use with some Western air forces to the present day. The German Luftwaffe did not retire its last Phantom IIs until 2013. By the time production ended in October 1979, McDonnell and licensees had built 5,201 aircraft in fourteen different versions.

THE END OF INDEPENDENCE

Donald Douglas Sr. had been regarded as a pillar of the American aviation industry for decades. He had successfully led his company through the recession of 1939, built it back up during the war years, and after the Second World War made it the undisputed market leader in the production of passenger aircraft. Donald Douglas Sr. was a company patriarch of the old school, who preferred to take

This photo shows the transport of the full-size mockup of the Skylab space laboratory, developed and built by McDonnell, aboard a Boeing Super Guppy aircraft. The first manned American space station circled the earth from its launch into space on May 14, 1973, until it burned up in an intentional reentry into the earth's atmosphere on July 11, 1979, after having fulfilled its function and no longer being needed. NASA

In the mid-1990s, McDonnell Douglas took part in an invitation to tender from NASA for Project X-33, a vertical-takeoff-and-landing reusable space transport. On July 2, 1996, however, Lockheed Martin was declared the winner, and the McDonnell Douglas entry proceeded no further than computer graphics such as this one. *NASA / Computer graphic by J. Frassanito & Associates*

the destiny of his world company into his own hands by telephone rather than delegate tasks to his subordinates. His son Donald Douglas Jr., who took over direction of the company in 1957, was quite different, and his aggressive leadership style resulted in an exodus of talented employees from the company's management. After Douglas Jr. and his father, who remained chairman of the supervisory board and thus continued to have a leadership role within the company, hesitated in deciding to make a start in the jet age, Boeing gained a two-year lead, which resulted in sales figures

for the Douglas DC-8 lagging behind. As well, unlike Douglas, Boeing was able to cross-finance its 707 by way of military contracts for the KC-135 sister project. Plagued by heavy losses from the DC-8 project, at the beginning of the 1960s the company was saved from an early end only by its profitable spaceflight division. Douglas had better luck with the DC-9, for which Boeing initially had no answer. Riding this wave of success, Douglas expanded DC-9 production capacities so greatly, however, that the selling of DC-9s below manufacturing cost to boost demand developed into a loss-making venture. Historical sources say that Douglas lost about 1.25 million dollars on each of the first twenty aircraft built! Instead of earning well on its bestseller and building up a financial buffer for future projects such as the DC-10, which was appearing on the horizon, in 1966 Douglas slid deep into the red.

The situation was so dramatic that the company urgently needed an external financial injection in order to survive. While searching for a straw to grasp, father and son initially approached financial investors and held discussions with the Rockefeller family and the eccentric tycoon Howard Hughes. These efforts failed, however, leaving a merger with an economically sounder company as the only way out. The who's who of the American aviation industry, including North American and General Dynamics, initially showed interest, but in the end only McDonnell was left as a potential merger candidate. After James Smith McDonnell purchased 300,000 Douglas shares on the stock market in 1967, leaving just 9,000 shares held by father and son Douglas, on January 13, 1967, the Douglas supervisory board declared itself ready to merge with McDonnell.

The new McDonnell Douglas Aircraft Company, with the independent branches McDonnell Aircraft Company, Douglas Aircraft Company, and McDonnell Douglas Astronautics Company, was launched on April 27, 1967. Company headquarters was set up in the former McDonnell factory in St. Louis, Missouri, where James Smith McDonnell resided as chairman and CEO. Donald Douglas Sr., then seventy-four years old, was named honorary chairman of the

In October 1980, the American air force organized the competition for a medium-size transport aircraft originally designated the Cargo Experimental (CX) program, to supplement the existing C-5A Galaxy and C-141 Starlifter. On August 28, 1981, the Douglas Long Beach Division of McDonnell Douglas was given the task of developing and producing the resulting C-17 Globemaster III. The transport was conceived for use with a minimum crew of two pilots and a loadmaster. After the merger with Boeing, the project continued as the Boeing C-17. The photo shows an "elephant walk," a USAF term for a formation taxi, in this case by twelve KC-10s and six C-17s of the 305th Air Mobility Wing at McGuire Air Force Base in Lakehurst, New York. *US Air Force / Russ Meseroll*

supervisory board, while his then-forty-seven-year-old son continued to head the company's Douglas division, based in Long Beach. McDonnell's legendary patriarchal leadership style was preserved. He spoke to his employees daily, using a loudspeaker system installed in the factory: "This is Mac calling all the team" rang through the halls and offices of the McDonnell factory in St. Louis.

At the time of the merger with Douglas, McDonnell, unlike his merger partner, was able to make a profit of forty-three million dollars with sales figures from both companies. The newly created company was a perfect symbiosis, since, in contrast to the later takeover by Boeing in 1997, there were no competing aircraft projects within the combine.

And so, even on the DC-10 project, Douglas and McDonnell pulled on the same string, and two months after the Lockheed L-1011 was launched, they gave their approval to production and active sales of the DC-10 to the airlines. At the same time, the McDonnell branch in St. Louis secured the future of the air and space company, with military products such as the F-15 Eagle, AV-8 Harrier, and F/A-18 Hornet, while Douglas continued development of the civil model palette around the MD-80/90 and MD-11.

Donald Douglas Sr. and James Smith McDonnell remained active in the company until their deaths. McDonnell died on August 22, 1980, and Donald Douglas Sr. followed him a short time later on February 1, 1981. America said goodbye to the last two great patriarchs of the US aviation industry.

CHAPTER 3
ON THE WAY
TO THE DC-10
THE FIRST WIDE-BODY JETS

THE FIRST FOUR WIDE-BODY JETS—THE BOEING 747, MCDONNELL DOUGLAS DC-10, LOCKHEED L-1011, AND AIRBUS A300—ENTERED SCHEDULED SERVICE AT THE BEGINNING OF THE 1970S.

The history of the wide-body jet goes back to two major events in 1964 and 1965. While airlines around the world were still busy trying to compensate for the enormous losses caused by the start of the jet age, Pan Am founder and owner Juan Trippe had something even bigger in mind. Like most airlines around the world, his was struggling with the overcapacities resulting from the introduction of the Boeing 707 and Douglas DC-8. The jets were twice as fast and had four times the seating capacity of the propeller airliners they had replaced. As if that was not enough, the long-range piston-engine airliners developed at the end of the 1950s, such as the DC-7C and L-1649A, had become worthless almost overnight with the advent of the jet age. After all, who wanted to fly in the comparatively slow propeller airliners, which flew through the weather, when a more comfortable alternative was available in the fast jets, which glided through the stratosphere?

The maiden flight of the Boeing 747 prototype on February 9, 1969, introduced the age of the jumbo jet. *Author's archive*

TOP Pan Am president Juan T. Trippe signed a memorandum of understanding for twenty-five Boeing 747s on December 22, 1965. This may be considered the official hour of birth of the jumbo jet. *Author's archive*

BOTTOM Pan Am set up a comfortable lounge in the upper deck of the Boeing 747 so that its first-class passengers could dine exclusively above the clouds. This unique experience could be experienced by anyone in January 2019, in a perfectly re-created cabin of a Pan Am Boeing 747 in Los Angeles. *Pan American Experience by Air Hollywood*

In the midst of this painful upheaval, Trippe was already planning the next step toward a passenger jet that would be more than twice as large—the Boeing 747. He challenged the Boeing management, promising an initial order for twenty-five of these jumbo jets should the manufacturer guarantee to build them. In parallel with these business games, the leading American aircraft makers were invited by the US Air Force to participate in an invitation to tender for a transport aircraft called the C-5A, with a then-unimaginable payload of more than 110 tons. Boeing, Douglas, and Lockheed all accepted the challenge and submitted their designs. Although Boeing was initially considered the sure winner, Lockheed was ultimately awarded the contract to design and produce the C-5A, which was given the name Galaxy.

But Boeing was not to come away entirely empty-handed and was "compensated" with a memorandum of understanding from Pan American for twenty-five Boeing 747s, which was signed on December 22, 1965. Both projects, airframe and engines, were started at the same time. This was a first in civil aviation; normally, engine development is years ahead of airframe development. When Boeing selected the Pratt & Whitney JT9D, the engine existed only on the paper of the Pratt & Whitney designers. The same was true of the high-bypass-ratio (8:1) General Electric TF39 turbofan engine, which Lockheed chose to power the Galaxy and from which the civil CF6 engine was derived.

Two point five was the magic formula in the course of 747 development. Compared to the preceding 707 model, it was supposed to be capable of transporting 2.5 times as many passengers. Pratt & Whitney developed for it an engine with 2.5 times the thrust of the most powerful civil jet engine of the day. Although the Boeing 747 came from a blank sheet of paper and had no design parallels to the proposed C-5A design, the project profited from the engine maker's preliminary work for what later became the US Air Force transport known as the Galaxy.

Takeoff by a former Pam Am Boeing 747SP-21 for a nonstop flight from New York's John F. Kennedy Airport to Tokyo, shortly after United Air Lines took over the aircraft as part of a package that included Pan Am's Pacific routes. The aircraft is still wearing the original paint scheme of its previous owner, supplemented by the provisionally applied name of its new owner. *Jon Proctor*

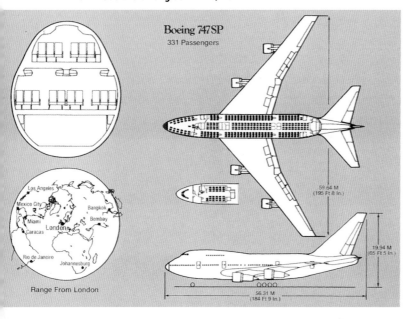

Boeing 747SP
331 Passengers

Los Angeles
Mexico City
Bangkok
Miami
Bombay
Caracas
London
Rio de Janeiro
Johannesburg

Range From London

59.64 M
(195 Ft 8 In.)

19.94 M
(65 Ft 5 In.)

56.31 M
(184 Ft 9 In.)

TOP This drawing shows an example of the possible first- and economy-class seating of the Boeing 747SP and its enormous range potential, which, for example, enabled flights from London to Los Angeles with full payload.

BOTTOM The reliability of the L-1011 and the passenger comfort offered onboard the large-capacity jet helped the charter airline LTU of Dusseldorf earn its outstanding reputation.

Final assembly at Everett began in September 1967 with the arrival of the first nose section, completed in Boeing's Wichita factory. The next milestone occurred in March 1968, when the first wing was removed from the assembly jig. The aircraft was moving irresistibly toward completion, but at that time not a single Pratt & Whitney JT9D engine had as yet run on the test bench. Not until June 1968 could a JT9D be tested in its future element for the first time, not on a 747 but under the wing of a Boeing B-52 experimental aircraft.

And so Boeing presented its new pride and joy to the public at the official rollout on September 30, 1968, still without functioning power plants. The aircraft systems were activated in the prototype, with the fitting registration N7470, for the first time in January 1969, and the functioning of the undercarriage and the control surfaces and flaps was tested. On February 9, Boeing test pilot Jack Waddell was so satisfied with the technical state of the plane, nicknamed City of Everett, that he decided that the day of its maiden flight had come. Immediately after the landing, still standing at the foot of the aircraft stairs, when asked for his initial impressions the effusive Waddell declared, "The aircraft flies like a pilot's dream."

While Boeing was busy with construction of the first 747 prototype, the company McDonnell Douglas, created in 1967 after the merger of Douglas and McDonnell, announced that it would produce a trijet for medium- and long-range routes. Once again it was American Airlines, which after the DC-3 and DC-7 now became the launch customer for the third airliner of the legendary DC family of aircraft, the DC-10. On February 2, 1968, American signed an order for twenty-five DC-10-10 aircraft, with options for another twenty-five. The first DC-10 flew on August 29, 1970—just three months before the at-first-glance-similar Lockheed L-1011 TriStar, which took to the air for the first time on November 16, 1970, at Lockheed's airfield at Burbank, California. In contrast to its Lockheed colleagues, from the outset the McDonnell Douglas engineers envisaged the use of engines from different manufacturers for its DC-10.

This photo was taken from a cabin window of the first L-1011 destined for TWA, on the morning of May 10, 1972, as the aircraft taxied past a row of Eastern Airlines TriStars while on its way to the runway for its delivery flight to Kansas City. *Jon Proctor*

McDonnell Douglas was thus spared the drama that brought Lockheed almost to the brink of ruin after the temporary insolvency of the British engine maker Rolls-Royce. While its RB.211 engine, offered exclusively for the L-1011, was technically superior to the American products from General Electric and Pratt & Whitney, as a result of Rolls-Royce's temporary insolvency, delivery of the first L-1011 was delayed until 1972. Lockheed thus fell far behind McDonnell Douglas, whose first two DC-10 production aircraft were simultaneously delivered to American and United Airlines.

In addition to the American manufacturers Boeing, Lockheed, and McDonnell Douglas, the European Airbus consortium was working on a fourth jumbo jet, which was supposed to begin flying in the early 1970s. The European dream began to take shape in 1965, true to the motto "together we are strong," with the objective of pitting itself against the previously dominant American aviation industry. No European aircraft producer and no nation would have been in a position financially and organizationally to handle a project the size of Airbus. The opportunity that existed could therefore succeed only at the European level. In its founding years the Airbus was the key project, both politically and economically, for the slowly coalescing western Europe.

The blending of economy and politics and the consideration of national sensitivities led to an extremely complex Airbus company structure. On the basis of a government agreement between France and Germany on May 29, 1969, which the Netherlands joined in 1970, in the beginning the tone of Airbus was not that of an aircraft maker but rather of a joint government committee. The governments gave this organ, which reported on the technical, industrial, commercial, and financial progress of the program, control over tasks that fell to it within the program. The government committee in turn formed an executive committee, which administered tasks given by the government committee and to which a member of each government belonged. Both committees could make use of state administrative bodies, which appeared under the title "managing organ." The corporate group Société Nationale Industrielle Aérospatiale (SNIAS), from France, and the Deutsche Airbus GmbH, based in Munich, controlled development and production of the A300B via Airbus Industrie (AI), which was based in Paris and later Toulouse. AI was not, however, a conventional company like a stock company or limited-liability company; rather, it was an economic-interest grouping, or groupement d'interet economique according to French law. September 26, 1972, was a big day for Airbus. At the official rollout the consortium was finally able to present to the assembled representatives of the press, potential customers, and politicians of the partner nations not just drawings and models but the first of two A300B1 prototypes, a real aircraft they could touch. But it was not until the maiden flight on October 28 of that year that the dream of a European wide-body jet became a reality. Onboard this history-making flight were pilot Max Fischl (Airbus chief test pilot), copilot Bernard Ziegler, and flight test engineers Pierre Canell, Romeo Zinzoni, and Günter Scherer. After an extensive flight test program involving four aircraft—the two B1 prototypes and two B2 production aircraft—on March 15, 1974, the A300B became the first aircraft ever to simultaneously receive German and French type certifications. The American FAA followed with its certification two months later.

Engineers of the Lufthansa Technical Department played a major role in designing the cockpit of the Boeing 747-400 and made a significant contribution to this bestselling version of the aircraft. *Boeing*

Already fitted with the stairs leading to the upper deck, the nose section of the first 747-8 Intercontinental for Lufthansa is on its way for final assembly in the Everett factory. *Boeing*

The 747-8 in the new livery introduced by the German airline in 2018. *Lufthansa*

CHAPTER 4
ON THE WAY
TO THE DC-10
TWO ARE ONE TOO MANY

When C. R. Smith, president of American Airlines, signaled interest in a new jumbo jet with a seating capacity between the Boeing 707 and 747, McDonnell Douglas was not alone in seeing its chance to launch a new aircraft program. This potential contract also attracted the attention of Lockheed, based in Burbank, California. The company saw it as an opportunity to return to the civil aircraft market, which Lockheed had last served in the 1950s with propeller-driven aircraft: the piston-engined L-1049 Super Constellation and L-1649 Starliner and the four-engined L-188 Electra turboprop.

The market experts from McDonnell Douglas and Lockheed reckoned on a global contract volume for their almost identical designs, which would make it economically worthwhile to produce both types. When the last of 250 L-1011s to be built were delivered in 1984, and the last of 446 completed DC-10s in July 1989, it became apparent that the world market had been too small for two jets of this size.

The question "What if?" arose about both types. How many jets would Lockheed have been able to sell had Rolls-Royce, the exclusive maker of TriStar engines, not declared bankruptcy immediately after the prototype's maiden flight, and newly built L-1011s had not sat engineless for about a year on the Lockheed company airfield? And how many DC-10s could have been sold if the type's reputation had not been damaged by an unprecedented series of accidents beginning in 1972?

While Lockheed finally withdrew from the civil aircraft market in 1984, in the early 1990s McDonnell Douglas tried to position a follow-up model, the MD-11, on the market to compete against the then-new Airbus types A330/340 and the Boeing 777. After just 200 examples were built, Boeing, which had acquired McDonnell Douglas in 1997, halted production of the last big trijet in 2001. The MD-11's lack of success was in part responsible for the company, whose roots went back to 1921, being taken over by its fiercest competitor after seventy-six years.

Although very similar in their basic design, the DC-10 and L-1011 differed in many solutions for technical features. This photo shows the L-1011 prototype after returning to the Lockheed company airfield at Palmdale on November 16, 1970, immediately after its successful two-hour maiden flight. *Jon Proctor*

Pan Am used its twelve L-1011-500s on those routes for which its Boeing 747s were too large. *Author's archive*

Delta Air Lines was actually a customer for the L-1011, but due to delays in deliveries of the type, between 1972 and 1975 it had to lease five DC-10-10s to bridge the waiting period. Shown here is N603DA, lifting off from New York's La Guardia Airport for Atlanta in the late afternoon sun in February 1973. *Jon Proctor*

CHAPTER 5
MCDONNELL
DOUGLAS DC-10
THE MOST SUCCESSFUL TRIJET

Following the merger of Douglas and McDonnell, McDonnell Douglas, now one of the largest aviation and space businesses in the world, had sufficient capital to launch its planned DC-10 jumbo jet. The unanimous opinion in the industry was that without it, the company had no chance of surviving in the civil aircraft field. On April 25, 1968, McDonnell Douglas officially announced that it planned to produce the DC-10 and resume development work, which had been halted due to a shortage of capital. With the first fixed contracts from the US companies American Airlines, United Airlines, Northwest Orient Airlines, and Trans International, by the end of 1969 the Douglas Division already had 184 orders on the books, and the amortization of the development costs for the new trijet, in excess of one billion dollars, seemed to move close at hand. Thus highly motivated, the McDonnell Douglas team made preparations for quantity production, whose interim high point was the prototype's maiden flight on August 29, 1970. It was followed

Swissair, together with SAS and KLM, was the launch customer for the long-range DC-10-30, recognizable by the third main undercarriage unit on the fuselage centerline. *ETH-Bibliothek Zurich, Swissair*

Loading a DC-10 freighter of the express company FedEx at its central American hub in Memphis, Tennessee. *Author's archive*

by a comprehensive flight test program, in which the DC-10 was taken to its structural limits and whose crowning achievement was the awarding of American type certification on May 24, 1971.

Douglas had selected three General Electric CF6-6D turbofan engines as standard power plants for the DC-10, but airline customers could also opt for Pratt & Whitney JT9D or Rolls-Royce RB.211 engines. It is an interesting fact that not only Lufthansa's engineering directorate but also that of United Air Lines favored the competing Lockheed L-1011, but both were forced to yield to the sales departments of their respective airlines, which preferred the DC-10. And so, when McDonnell Douglas handed the first two aircraft over to its first customers in an official ceremony on July 29, 1971, a DC-10 in United colors sat parked beside one destined for American Airlines. Just eight days later, American opened another chapter in the story of the DC-10 with the first scheduled commercial flight by the type. By that time, McDonnell Douglas was already hard at work on further versions of its wide-body jet. On February 28, 1972, the manufacturer launched the DC-10-20, the first version equipped with Pratt & Whitney JT9D engines. At the urging of the first American customer, Northwest Orient Airlines, the designation of this version was changed to DC-10-40 before the first aircraft was delivered, so as to create the impression of a more advanced model among the traveling public. Both Northwest and Japan Airlines chose the Pratt & Whitney JT9D turbofan to power its DC-10-40s, the same engine that powered their Boeing 747 fleets, in order to reduce maintenance and spares costs. The biggest difference between it and the DC-10-10 was the DC-10-40 version's significantly greater range. Outwardly, the subtype could be identified by a third main undercarriage unit on the fuselage centerline to better distribute the aircraft's greater weight during takeoff and landing. This feature was also present on the DC-10-30, which first flew on June 21, 1972. Powered by CF6-50C engines, this variant was initiated by a major order from the KSSU consortium, made up of KLM, SAS, Swissair, and UTA, on June 9, 1969. Significant customers for this version of the DC-10, 163 examples of which were built, included the European carriers Alitalia, Iberia, Lufthansa, and Sabena, which were members of the ATLAS consortium. Like the KSSU airlines, they shared maintenance responsibilities and set common technical and operational standards, and not just for their DC-10 fleets.

Aeromexico and Mexicana Airlines, on the other hand, decided on the DC-10-15, the first example of which was delivered in June 1981. This hot and high version of the wide-body jet was equipped with the more powerful engines of the DC-10-30 version to allow operations from airports with high elevations and outside air temperatures, but it had the lighter fuselage of the DC-10-10.

In 1981, McDonnell Douglas handed the first DC-10-30ER (extended range), with an additional fuel tank in the fuselage, over to its first customer, Finnair. The addition of the extra fuel tank came at the cost of payload, but it increased the DC-10's range to 6,835 miles.

OVERVIEW OF DC-10 VARIANTS

DC-10-10

The DC-10-10 was initially conceived for American domestic routes, but during its career it was also operated to other continents; for example, by Turkish Airlines, based in Istanbul. A total of 122 examples of this subtype were built.

The DC-10-10CF Convertible Freighter combi version of the DC-10 base model had a side-mounted cargo door on the main deck and a reinforced cabin floor. It could be used either as a pure freighter or passenger aircraft—but it could also be employed in a mixed combi layout.

DC-10-20/40

Long-range version of the DC-10 powered by Pratt & Whitney JT9D engines. Only Northwest Orient Airlines and Japan Airlines ordered examples of this series, which was originally called the DC-10-20. At the urging of Northwest, however, it was given the type designation DC-10-40, which sounded more advanced.

DC-10-30

The most successful DC-10 version, with 163 examples built, it was offered only with General Electric CF6-50 turbofan engines and, after the Version 40, was the second-longest-range subtype of the DC-10. It was available from the manufacturer as a pure passenger airliner, as a DC-10-30CF combi version, as a DC-10-30AF freighter, or as the extended-range DC-10-30ER.

DC-10-15

This special version of the DC-10-10, developed specially for high and hot airfields, was equipped with the more powerful CF6-50 engines from the DC-10-30. In combination with the lower structural weight of the DC-10-10, it had excellent takeoff characteristics, even under hot and high conditions. The Mexican airlines Mexicana and Aeromexico were the only customers, purchasing seven examples that were delivered from 1981 onward.

KC-10A

Military version for the US Air Force, based on the DC-10-30AF. McDonnell Douglas built sixty examples of the KC-10A, which in addition to transport duties serves as an air-refueling tanker. Two further examples were produced for the Royal Netherlands Air Force as the KDC-10-30CF by converting two former DC-10-30CFs of the Dutch charter airline Martinair Holland.

While the Canadian national carrier, Air Canada, chose the competing L-1011, privately owned Canadian Airlines operated fourteen McDonnell Douglas DC-10-10, -30, and -30F aircraft on its network of routes, which included Frankfurt. *Author's archive*

A Sabena DC-10-30F takes off from Brussels-Zaventem. *Sabena*

Sabena's DC-10 combis could carry freight in the forward fuselage and passengers in a cabin in the rear, separated from the cargo hold by a partition. *Sabena*

LN-RKA Olav Viking was one of five DC-10-30s ordered by SAS directly from McDonnell Douglas. In the 1980s, the fleet was expanded to twelve aircraft by acquiring used examples, including aircraft from KLM, Laker Airways, and Thai International. SAS

Thanks to the aircraft's large fuselage cross section, standard air freight containers could be transported in the below-floor cargo hold. SAS

Ask for it by number.

10 is such a nice round number,
it will be easy for you
to remember. Air travelers who
do remember the "10"
come to know a very special
kind of comfort, style and grace.
Number yourself among them
next time you fly.

"Book me aboard a 10... a DC-10."

MCDONNELL DOUGLAS

Advertisement for the McDonnell Douglas Aircraft Company.
Dave Robinson collection

Fuel miser DC-10.

CAB data on wide-body direct operating costs show
that the DC-10 is the most economical wide-cabin
jetliner for virtually any medium to long range route.

With its advanced wing, the DC-10 cruises thriftily
at Mach 0.82 to 0.87. Engine pylons, designed and
placed to minimize aerodynamic interference, are
carefully mated to fuel-efficient GE or Pratt &
Whitney high by-pass engines. The DC-10's clean,
low drag design minimizes the use of drag
inducing trim surfaces.

And the DC-10's straight through aft
engine nacelle is more than just a hallmark.
It's engineered that way to reduce
inlet air flow distortion.

The DC-10:
engineered to squeeze maximum
mileage from a pound of fuel.

The DC-10
MCDONNELL DOUGLAS

The DC-10's turbofan engines, among the most advanced at the time, made it
an economical and, in particular, quiet wide-body jet. *Dave Robinson collection*

The distinctive tail of the Swissair DC-10-30 was a familiar sight at the Zurich-Kloten airport for more than twenty years, from 1972 to 1992.
ETH-Bibliothek Zurich, Swissair

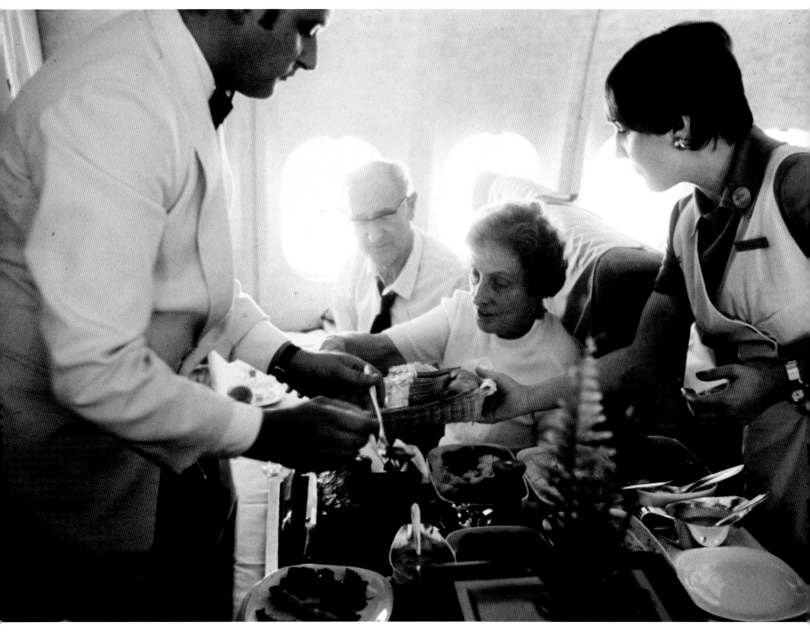

Opulent first-class service onboard a Swissair DC-10. *ETH-Bibliothek Zurich, Swissair*

In addition to Swissair, its vacation airline subsidiary Balair also operated the DC-10-30 on its network of routes. *Swissair*

The DC-10 cockpits of the airlines KLM, SAS, Swissair, and UTA of the KSSU consortium not only were 100 percent identical; they were also jointly defined by a KSSU team on behalf of the partners. Engine data were displayed on vertical-scale instruments, while other airlines selected round analog instruments.
ETH-Bibliothek Zurich, Swissair

Takeoff sequence by a Swissair DC-10 during the test program in the United States, prior to delivery to the Swiss airline. *ETH-Bibliothek Zurich, Swissair*

It was not suspected that this American Airlines DC-10-10 with the registration N110AA would be involved in one of the greatest catastrophes in civil aviation on May 25, 1979, when this photo of the aircraft was taken at Chicago's O'Hare Airport in April 1974. The disaster of flight AA 191—in which 273 people lost their lives within seconds after one of the aircraft's engines broke away and caused it to crash—is a constant reminder to the industry that in aviation, profits must never be put ahead of flight safety. *Jon Proctor*

People all over the world talk the same language about the DC-10: "I like it."

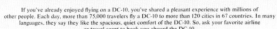

If you've already enjoyed flying on a DC-10, you've shared a pleasant experience with millions of other people. Each day, more than 75,000 travelers fly a DC-10 to more than 120 cities in 67 countries. In many languages, they say they like the spacious, quiet comfort of the DC-10. So, ask your favorite airline or travel agent to book you aboard the DC-10.

DC-10 the choice of 34 airlines

MCDONNELL DOUGLAS

DC-10-30
The 10th Dimension
Serving the Intercontinental network

Volume and capacity	Maximum volume	109 m³ (3,850 cu.ft.)
	Maximum payload	45,200 kg (99,440 lbs.)
	Maximum cargo payload with 50 % passenger load	
	CPH-SEA	22,600 kg (49,720 lbs.)
	TYO-(ANC)-CPH	29,600 kg (65,120 lbs.)
	CPH-BKK-SIN	15,000 kg (33,000 lbs.)
Pallets	LD-3	
	Liftainer	
	LD-7	

SAS CARGO

LEFT McDonnell Douglas tried to improve the image of the DC-10, which had been damaged by two spectacular crashes, through the "I like it" campaign. *Dave Robinson collection*

RIGHT DC-10: for SAS, the "tenth dimension." *SAS*

McDonnell Douglas used this DC-10-30CF, destined for World Airways and already painted in its colors, for advertising photos before it was delivered to American Airlines in March 1978. *Author's archive*

The photographer pressed his shutter release button a few seconds after liftoff by this DC-10-30 of American Trans Air (ATA) from Los Angeles airport in 2008. The airline ceased operating the same year. *Jon Proctor*

CHAPTER 6
MCDONNELL
DOUGLAS KC-10
THE FLYING FILLING STATION

In addition to 386 civil DC-10s, between 1981 and 1988, McDonnell Douglas also produced sixty military KC-10 Extender transport and aerial-refueling aircraft. This version is based on the civil DC-10-30CF combi freighter, with a side-mounted cargo door on the main deck and a reinforced cabin floor. For use as an aerial-refueling tanker, the KC-10 was equipped with a refueling boom, which military aircraft would engage to take on fuel. The aircraft of the US Air Force, designated the KC-10A, replaced some of its dated KC-135 tankers, which had been built in the 1950s and 1960s. McDonnell Douglas handed the first KC-10A over to the 32nd Aerial Refueling Squadron of Strategic Air Command in March 1981. One reason why the KC-10 was chosen was the then-still-good availability of DC-10 spare parts around the globe, which could also have been used for the military aircraft in an emergency.

An F-22 Raptor refueling from a KC-10 Extender of the 305th Air Mobility Wing of the US Air Force. *Staff Sgt. Andy M. Kin, US Air Force*

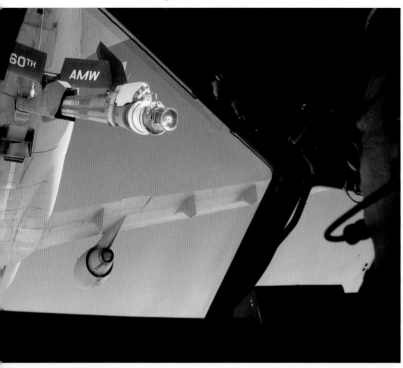

McDonnell Douglas hoped for a follow-up contract and possibly the complete replacement of the KC-135 by hundreds of KC-10 jets; however, production ended after sixty aircraft.

In addition, two DC-10-30CFs operated by Martin Air Holland were converted to KC-10 standard for the Royal Netherlands Air Force as KDC-10s. Omega Aerial Refueling Service also offers two other former civil DC-10s for commercial air-to-air refueling.

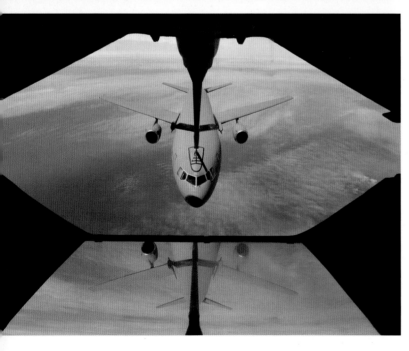

An F-22 Raptor refueling from a KC-10 Extender of the 305th Air Mobility Wing of the US Air Force. *Staff Sgt. Andy M. Kin, US Air Force*

A KC-10 Extender of the 305th Air Mobility Wing over the North Atlantic during a mission on March 18, 2016. *US Air National Guard / TSgt. Matt Hecht*

CHAPTER 7
MCDONNELL DOUGLAS DC-10 TANKER
IN USE AGAINST FOREST FIRES

The DC-10 air tanker has officially been certified by USFS, the American forestry service, as a fire-fighting aircraft since 2006. The converted former DC-10 passenger airliners are equipped with three tanks under the fuselage, which during a mission can discharge up to 35,500 liters (9,387 gal.) of extinguishing agents to fight forest fires and wildfires. The 10th Tanker Air Carrier had four converted DC-10-30s in use at the end of 2018, which were used mainly against fires in the state of California. One of the aircraft was, however, leased by the Australian authorities for the fire season there. A DC-10 tanker is usually flown by a crew of three, while a smaller pathfinder aircraft flies ahead of the DC-10 and leads the larger jet to the fire. Fire-extinguishing agents are usually dropped from a height of 197 to 328 feet at a speed of about 174 mph.

The external tanks mounted on an Air Tanker firefighting aircraft, a converted DC-10-30, contain 9,378 gallons of extinguishing agent. The California company 10 Tanker Air Carrier began investigating the possibility of a wide-body firefighting aircraft in 2002, which two years later culminated in the selection of the DC-10 as the jet best suited for this purpose. In March 2006, the FAA, the American regulatory body, issued a supplementary type certification for the modifications required to enable the DC-10 to carry the extinguishing agent. According to the operator, the DC-10 is well suited for this challenging role, primarily because of its robust structure. *10 Tanker Air Carrier*

These dramatic photos were not taken during a practice flight but during the Beacon fire. The DC-10 Air Tanker dropped extinguishing agent in support of 250 firefighters on the ground during the wildfire that raged north of San Francisco from August 27 to 29, 2011. This disastrous fire completely destroyed 1,767 acres of forest. The fire was brought under control in a relatively short time, thanks to the use of the DC-10 firefighting aircraft. *10 Tanker Air Carrier*

The DC-10 tankers undergo intensive maintenance during the night hours, when no firefighting missions can be flown on account of darkness. 10 Tanker Air Carrier employs a team of seven maintenance specialists for each aircraft. These teams follow the aircraft across the United States with equipment trucks filled with spare parts, when a return flight to home base does not seem practical for time and cost reasons. *10 Tanker Air Carrier*

CHAPTER 8
MCDONNELL
DOUGLAS MD-10
FROM FREIGHTER TO
FLYING EYE HOSPITAL

The MD-10 is not a new-build version of the DC-10, but rather the result of a modification program by McDonnell Douglas (MDC) and, after the merger, also by Boeing, with the goal of making existing DC-10s of all series more economical. Developed by MDC, the kit comprises primarily the installation of an advanced two-person glass cockpit identical to that of the MD-11, supplemented by further adaptations to reduce empty weight and fuel consumption. Another goal was to improve the reliability of various aircraft systems. After the program was first offered in 1996, both MDC and Boeing anticipated the largest modification program in the history of civil aviation, since at that time a total of 413 flying and parked DC-10s seemed predestined for conversion into MD-10s.

The express freight company FedEx, based in Memphis, Tennessee, did not wait long and in September 1996 became the first customer, with an initial fixed order for sixty MD-10s, which was soon increased to seventy-nine and finally eighty-nine aircraft. The jets selected for conversion were already part of the FedEx fleet and were flown to the Douglas Products Division of the Boeing factory for conversion from DC-10 to MD-10. The project was especially interesting for FedEx, since its pilots could now fly both the MD-10 and MD-11F, with the same type rating, and the flight engineer formerly required as third man in the cockpit was no longer needed.

The first FedEx DC-10 arrived at the modification factory in February 1997 and was turned into an MD-10, including a general overhaul, within 120 days. In contrast to other DC-10s that had previously served as freighters, FedEx had purchased these retired DC-10 passenger jets on the used-aircraft market only a short time before and had them converted by Boeing Airplane Services directly into MD-10 freighters. In addition to the standard MD-10 installations, such as the new cockpit, the total package included the installation of a 12-by-8.5-foot cargo door on the main deck, and conversion of the aircraft cabin for the future transport of freight pallets. In contrast to the DC-10 and early MD-11 freighters, the MD-10 for the first time has a fixed bulkhead between the freight compartment and nose section. This rigid barrier replaced the safety net previously installed, which was supposed to protect the crew from pallets and containers sliding forward in the event of a crash landing. In order to ensure that the net could stretch on landing, a safety zone had to be left, which was not economically useful. The MD-10 was different and, for example, allowed the installation of a small crew section in place of the earlier catchment zone, as well as the transport of additional freight pallets.

The first modified MD-10 was used for the certification program, involving approximately 800 test flights, which ended with certification by the American FAA on May 9, 2000. As hopefully as the MD-10 program began in 1996, its actual numbers were disappointing: the eighty-nine conversions ordered by FedEx were the only ones carried out, and Federal Express remained the sole customer for the modernized version of the DC-10. In June 2008, FedEx announced that its MD-10s had received a supplemental FAA certification for a head-up display (HUD). During the approach to land, information from the primary flight instruments was projected onto a glass panel before the pilot's eyes, which was in his forward field of view toward the runway. This indicator technology was combined with an Enhanced Flight Vision System, originally developed for the military for better vision in darkness and clouds. After the fleet had been completely reequipped in 2012, FedEx MD-10 crews could make out the approach and runway lighting in front of them, while crews of other aircraft still had no direct view of the ground.

McDonnell Douglas advertising brochure for the modernized version of the DC-10. Contrary to the high-flying hopes of the manufacturer, which dreamed of the biggest conversion program in the company's history, only FedEx warmed to the MD-10 program and remained its sole customer. *Author's archive*

In January 2019, the FedEx MD-10 fleet still consisted of thirty-four aircraft. One of these found a new owner in Transportes Aéreos Bolivianos, which became the second freight airline with an MD-10 in its fleet.

ORBIS: THE FLYING EYE HOSPITAL

A very special relationship has existed between Federal Express and Orbis for decades. The aid organization, which is active around the world and is funded by donations, has set itself the objective of treating eye disorders, even in countries without comprehensive medical care. To help on the spot, Orbis brings a complete eye hospital, installed in its jets, to people in need, especially in Asia, Africa, and Latin America. After having a Douglas DC-8-21 and a DC-10-10, its current MD-10 is already the third generation of aircraft used by Orbis. The jets are flown by active or former FedEx pilots who voluntarily fly for Orbis in their spare time. They are supported by many other FedEx employees on the ground, who ensure that the MD-10 operates smoothly. In 2011, the aircraft was donated by FedEx, along with a financial donation of more than five million dollars. In the years that followed, the Mobile Medical International Corporation, based in St. Johnsbury, Vermont, provided the components for a flying hospital including operating theater and training areas, in which eye specialists, who are also volunteers, mentor local doctors. Setting up a hospital on the ground is itself a complex task, but installing a complete eye clinic in a former cargo aircraft, with all the equipment and hygiene of a regular hospital, is a very special challenge. Under Orbis leadership, retired employees of FedEx and McDonnell Douglas found the optimal solution. Located on the main deck, the hospital is so designed that its individual components are mounted on aircraft pallets that can be placed onboard through the side cargo door. They can also be easily removed for prescribed aircraft maintenance. The side panels, treatment cabins, water and power supply, and medical apparatus are premounted in St. Johnsbury in nine large modules for the main deck and two work stations in the forward lower deck and are assembled onboard. Never before in the history of aviation was such a complex flying hospital conceived and certified.

In addition to the medical certification, the new flying eye hospital, which was converted in a hangar in Southern California, had to seek approval from the American FAA. The Orbis team carried out various test flights, with Eric van Court and Bob Moreau, one a retired FedEx pilot and the other active, at the controls of the trijet.

FACTS ABOUT ORBIS

- 39 million people on the earth are blind.
- 285 million people have visual impairment.
- Medical treatment would have made 80 percent of these visual impairments avoidable.
- Since 1982, Orbis has furthered the education of almost 350,000 eye doctors and treated the eye diseases of twenty-four million people in ninety-two countries.

The flying eye hospital takes off on its next mission. The MD-10 previously served with FedEx and was donated to Orbis in 2011. The conversion, which was completed in 2016, and the aircraft's certification as a flying hospital were financed by the express freight company. The organization also receives ongoing financial support from FedEx, whose employees, including pilots and mechanics, voluntarily operate the MD-10. © Orbis/NAsia

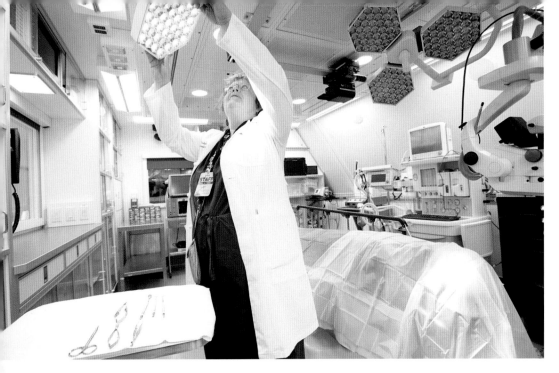

TOP The entire flying hospital onboard the MD-10, including its operating theater (*photo*), has the same equipment and hygiene standards as Western clinics. © *Orbis/NAsia*

BOTTOM Local eye specialists are given additional training onboard the Orbis MD-10 through the use of instructional films. © *Orbis/NAsia*

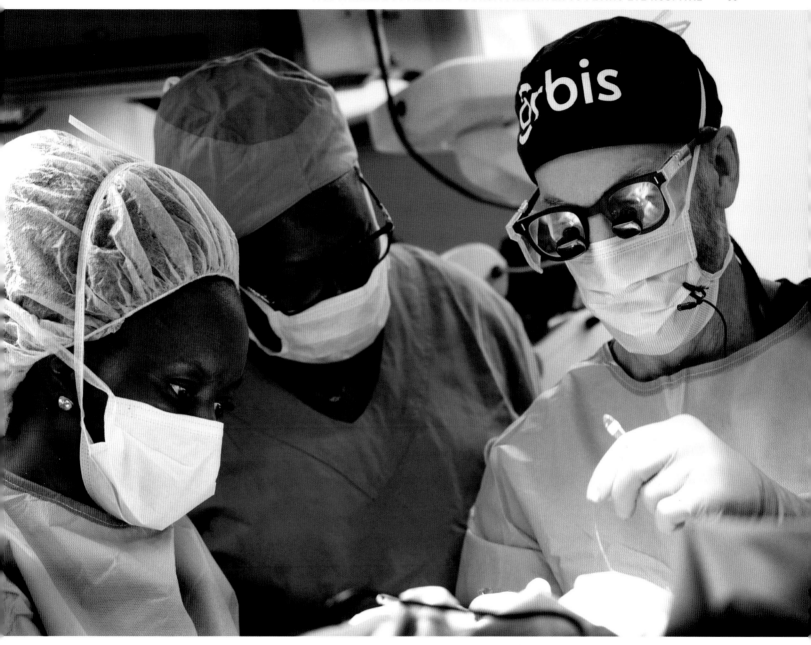

The eye specialists who accompany the aircraft work as volunteers for Orbis. © *Orbis / Geoff Bugbee*

CHAPTER 9
ON THE WAY
TO THE MD-11

DOUGLAS DC-10 SUPER 60

After expressions of interest by Air New Zealand and Swissair in the first half of the 1970s, McDonnell Douglas developed the DC-10 Super 60. Originally designated the Super 50, Douglas changed the designation for marketing reasons, following the lead of the successful stretched version of the four-jet DC-8.

The DC-10 Super 60 was supposed to be capable of carrying about 350 passengers in two classes—compared to the approximately 275 on the original DC-10-30—while its fuselage was lengthened by about 26.6 feet and its wings extended by 4.9 feet on each side. The extended wings were necessary in order to avoid any deterioration in the longer aircraft's takeoff characteristics compared to the standard DC-10. It was also planned to adapt the landing flaps to the new wing design, which was essentially based on the original DC-10 wing, and to introduce a conical rear fuselage.

The McDonnell Douglas engineers calculated that the extended DC-10 would consume about 24 percent less fuel than the base model. The cost per seat kilometer, it was expected, would be below that of the Boeing 747-200. After an expected formal program start in early 1979, the first DC-10 Super 60 was supposed to enter service with the first customers in 1982.

By 1979, plans were so far advanced that three concepts for different fuselage lengths for medium- and long-distance routes had been worked out—the DC-10-61, -62, and -63. It was also envisaged that the new DC-10 versions would be equipped with the then-available first-generation glass cockpits and use more light composite materials in their construction.

After various design studies, the final MD-11 design crystallized at the end of the 1980s. The drawing shown here was published by McDonnell Douglas before the first flight of the MD-11 prototype on January 10, 1990. *Author's archive*

The crash of American Airlines Flight 191 at Chicago O'Hare on May 25, 1979, and the subsequent grounding of the DC-10 fleet worldwide ended the dreams of the McDonnell Douglas team. The Super 60 project was abruptly canceled, since the type's reputation had been irreparably damaged and no airline wanted to invest in further versions of the DC-10.

Nevertheless, several design details of the Super 60 made their way into the DC-10-15 and DC-10-30ER versions, and thus the development work by the MDS engineers had not been totally in vain.

MD-100

In 1983, when the last DC-10s were leaving the assembly building in Long Beach at a rate of one aircraft per month, McDonnell Douglas (MDC) decided to attempt a revitalization of the program. The new design was to be no simple update of the DC-10 Super 60 from the 1970s; rather, it would incorporate entirely new technologies. An outward symbol of the new project was the use of the MD abbreviation. Nineteen years after the merger of Douglas and McDonnell, the McDonnell Douglas management believed that the time had come to undertake a corresponding amendment of the type designations of its civil aircraft program. A crucial factor may have been the crash of the American Airlines DC-10 in May 1979, which seriously damaged the abbreviation DC in the eyes of the public.

The MD-100 was planned with a modern two-man glass cockpit and was to be powered by three Pratt & Whitney PW4000 or General Electric CF6-80C2 turbofan engines. Externally the projected MD-100 differed from the DC-10 in having winglets on both wingtips, splayed outward by up to 15 degrees. MDC tested their effectiveness by experimentally installing winglets, which reduced drag and thus saved fuel, on the wingtips of a DC-10 of Continental Airlines. The tests, carried out in cooperation with NASA starting in August 1981, confirmed a fuel savings of approximately 3 percent. Like the earlier DC-10-60, the future version of the DC-10 was planned in different

versions. The MD-100-10, which was 4.9 feet shorter than the DC-10, was supposed to carry a maximum of 270 passengers. The MD-100-20, which was lengthened by 65.6 feet, was designed to carry up to 333 passengers. Also planned was an MD-100-20ER, with a maximum range of 8,078 miles. There was also an MD-100-20 in a combined freight-passenger version and an MD-100-30, which would be stretched by 39 feet compared to the DC-10. MDC hoped to deliver the first aircraft in 1989.

On November 11, 1983, however, the hopes of the project developer fizzled out, like they had for the DC-10-60, after MDC chairman Sanford N. McDonnell announced the immediate cancellation of the MD-100 project due to lack of customer interest.

MD-11X

In 1984, McDonnell Douglas for the first time released impressions of a successor to the DC-10, with the designation MD-11. The new design was shown in the MD-11X-10 and MD-11X-20 versions. The MD-11X-10, whose external dimensions were similar to those of the DC-10-30, would be powered by three General Electric CF6-80C2 or, alternatively, Pratt & Whitney PW4000 engines and have a maximum range of 7,456 miles. The MD-11X-20, which was stretched by 22.3 feet compared to the DC-10, had a capacity of about 330 passengers in a mixed version with first and economy class. The conical rear fuselage was very reminiscent of the MD-11 as actually built; however, this design still lacked the prominent fuel-saving winglets on the wingtips.

According to contemporaneous reports, this third precursor to the MD-11 was not brought to production standard because of a contract from the package and freight service Federal Express, which to the joy of McDonnell Douglas management ordered ten brand-new DC-10-30s for delivery by 1984. This gave MDC the time it needed to further tailor the final MD-11 design to meet the needs of potential customers.

CHAPTER 10
MCDONNELL DOUGLAS /
BOEING MD-11
THE ULTIMATE TRIJET

The McDonnell Douglas MD-11 was based on the original DC-10 design from the 1960s, but it was made fit for the future through the use of the most-modern systems and lightweight materials available at the time of its development. The manufacturer also added various aerodynamic improvements and more-efficient power plants, in order to sustainably reduce fuel consumption compared to its predecessors. The so-called glass cockpit of the MD-11, with its six Honeywell display screens in the main instrument panel, was one of the most modern installed in a civilian aircraft in the 1980s. In combination with an advanced flight management system, it made the flight engineer required as a third crewman in the cockpit of the DC-10 redundant.

The numbers presented by McDonnell Douglas (MDC) at the end of 1988 sounded hopeful. There were committed orders for eighty-eight MD-11s on the order books—about a year before the planned first flight of the new trijet. The cushion of orders, which just a short time later had climbed to about 250, caused the leadership in Long Beach, California, to dream of raising the production rate to four jets per month by 1991. The first flight, on January 10, 1990, was followed by a test program involving five aircraft, which ended on November 8, 1990, with certification by the Federal Aviation Administration (FAA). The MD-11 and MD-11F were entered in its type certificate sheet as modernized versions of the DC-10. The MD-11 was also the first type certified by the then newly created JAA, the European regulatory authority, on behalf of its member states in November 1991—one year after the FAA.

At the end of the certification program, McDonnell Douglas estimated its cost at about 3.3 billion dollars. This was a considerable sum, which had to be earned back before the program could begin, to say nothing of make a profit. But the MD-11 did not have what McDonnell Douglas had promised its customers. This devastating news was first announced by an angry American Airlines president Robert Crandall following delivery of the first MD-11s to his airline. Put in a nutshell: the MD-11 used too much fuel. With a full payload, instead of the promised 8,077 miles it flew just 7,456 miles, while for example on its predestined route from Hong Kong to Los Angeles, it could have carried just seventy-seven passengers. The reasons for the performance shortcomings were complex and were partly due to the unexpectedly high fuel consumption of the General Electric and Pratt & Whitney engines and partly to excessive airframe drag. The problem had appeared during the certification flights, and for a time McDonnell Douglas contemplated designing a completely new wing for the MD-11, but this would have resulted in unacceptable delays and cost increases for the project. Although McDonnell Douglas worked closely with NASA in an effort to improve the aircraft's aerodynamics, and proposed a comprehensive package of measures to remedy its shortcomings, at the time of its introduction to the market, the MD-11 was infamous in airline circles as a "gas guzzler." Notwithstanding this, the makers of the engines and airframe worked feverishly to find solutions, which in 1991 did in fact lead to improved performance by the turbofan engines and reduced airframe drag. The latter was achieved with three packages, which McDonnell Douglas offered for installation on aircraft already delivered, and installed in new aircraft at the factory. The improvements primarily involved aerodynamic changes to the slats and ailerons, engine pylons, and elevator. As an interim solution, McDonnell Douglas offered to install an auxiliary fuel tank in the fuselage to enable the aircraft to achieve the contractually guaranteed range—albeit at the cost of cargo capacity in the lower deck.

TOP In January 2019, Lufthansa Cargo maintained the largest fleet of MD-11F freighters after Federal Express and UPS. *Lufthansa Cargo*

BOTTOM Taiwanese EVA Air Cargo was one of the many airlines around the globe that operated brand-new and converted MD-11F freighters. *Author's archive*

Frankfurt was one of the VARIG destinations to which the former Brazilian airline operated its passenger versions of the MD-11. *Dr. John Provan*

Singapore Airlines (SIA) in particular was directly affected by the MD-11's inadequate range, which prevented it from making nonstop flights from Singapore to London with a worthwhile payload—which is precisely why SIA had ordered this type. It wasn't long before the Asian airline canceled its order for up to twenty aircraft and selected the Airbus A340-300 as an alternative. McDonnell Douglas fought vehemently to retain such a significant contract and even offered to extend the MD-11's wingspan as a solution to the problem, but SIA had lost patience and, much to the joy of the Europeans, switched to their four-engined long-range product. Other airlines also baled out, and not just because of the MD-11's performance problems, since Operation Desert Storm began on January 16, 1991, plunging the world economy (including the airline business) into one of its greatest crises. Instead of ordering new aircraft, many airlines reduced their activities and parked some of their jets in the desert—waiting for better times.

Instead of a comfortable order cushion of 357 declarations of intent, by the time the first MD-11 was delivered in November 1990, just 200 aircraft left the final-assembly line in Long Beach before production ended in January 2001. For McDonnell Douglas the MD-11 had become a financial flop, which decisively contributed to the end of the tradition-steeped aircraft maker.

Entirely in the tradition of the early types from the Douglas civil aircraft division, from the beginning McDonnell Douglas offered the MD-11 as a pure passenger jet, as a freight-passenger combine, as a pure freighter, and, starting in August 1991, as the MD-11CF Convertible Freighter. The first customer for the last mentioned, which could be converted from a pure cargo aircraft into a pure passenger jet in a short time, was the Dutch charter airline Martinair Holland.

For production of the MD-11, the final-assembly line for the DC-10—production of which ended in December 1988 in favor of its successor—was modified accordingly. Like comparable aircraft projects of this size, the share of the MD-11 components made in Long Beach was relatively small. McDonnell Douglas Canada built the complete wings, while General Electric Convair Division delivered the greater part of the fuselage structure to California. The conical rear fuselage was produced by Mitsubishi in Japan, the vertical tail and control surfaces by Alenia in Italy. CASA of Spain delivered the horizontal tail surfaces to Long Beach.

The horizontal tail is a good example of how, with relatively small but effective changes, McDonnell Douglas developed the DC-10 into the MD-11. The MD-11's tail surfaces were reduced in size by 17 percent compared to those of its predecessor, which led to a reduction in structural weight. At first glance, lengthening the fuselage forward of the wing while simultaneously reducing the area of the compensating horizontal tail and its control surfaces does not sound like a good idea, but the MD-11 had "relaxed stability," which enabled a Longitudinal Stability Augmentation System (LSAS) to ensure flight stability about the longitudinal axis. For example, computers ensured via automatic-control surface deflections that the aircraft remained at a prescribed angle of attack set by the pilot—even with the smaller tail. LSAS was also the protective mechanism against an excessive angle of attack during touchdown on the runway and liftoff, preventing the tail of the aircraft from contacting the runway, which might otherwise be a danger. Since for aerodynamic reasons the MD-11 tended to raise its nose after the main undercarriage touched down and when the air brakes on the upper surface of the wing were extended, the LSAS automatically moved the elevators to force the nose down. Like all the control surface movements carried out automatically by the

Ramp scene at Amsterdam-Schiphol airport in the 1990s. The MD-11 illustrated here, with the name Florence Nightingale, was selected by KLM for the last three excursion flights carrying MD-11 enthusiasts before it was flown to an American aircraft boneyard and stripped of all recyclable parts. *Author's archive*

MD-11 Freighter

TECHNOLOGY FOR THE 21ST CENTURY

MCDONNELL DOUGLAS

MD-11 COMBI

DESIGN DATA

Engines	3	CF6-80C2 or PW4460
Length	(ft/m)	201.3 / 61.4
Wingspan	(ft/m)	169.8 / 51.8
Fuel Capacity	(lb/kg)	258,721 / 117,354
MTOGW*	(lb/kg)	630,500 / 285,990
MLW*	(lb/kg)	481,500 / 218,405
MZFW*	(lb/kg)	451,300 / 204,706
OEW	(lb/kg)	286,131 / 129,787
Cargo Volume	(ft³/m³)	8,754 / 247.9
Net Space-Limited Payload at 8.5 lb/ft³ (136 kg/m³)**	(lb/kg)	110,645 / 50,188
Range at 111,164 lb (50,423 kg) (n mi / km)		5,640 / 10,445
Interior Floor Width	(in./cm)	220 / 559

* Optional
** 963 ft³ Lower Hold Baggage Allowance Based on 214-Passenger Configuration

CARGO CAPABILITY

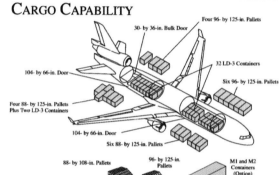

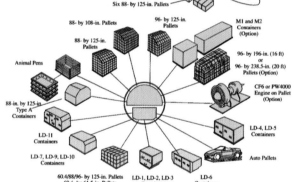

MAIN DECK FLEXIBLE PASSENGER/CARGO MIX

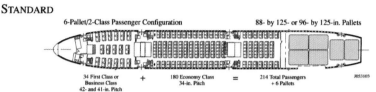

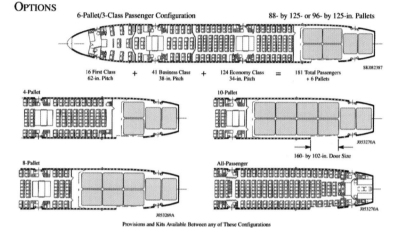

Provisions and Kits Available Between any of These Configurations

CARGO VOLUMES   Shown In Ft³ (Number of Units)

LOWER DECK

	LD-3	88- by 125-in.	96- by 125-in.
Fwd	2,844 (18)	2,232 (6)	2,442 (6)
Center	2,212 (14)	1,804 (4)*	1,628 (4)
Aft Bulk	510	510	510
Total Volume	5,566	4,546	4,580

* Four plus Two LD-3s Containers

MAIN DECK

No. of Pallets	88- by 125-in. Pallets	96- by 125-in. Pallets
6 (Standard)	3,342	3,590
4 (Option)	2,224	2,400
8 (Option)	4,460	4,780
10 (Option)	5,578	5,970

TECHNOLOGY FOR THE 21ST CENTURY

C0194

The material presented in this document is provided to acquaint you with the general characteristics of our products; it is not an offer and does not constitute a commitment, a warranty, or a representation. The detail specification, which is part of the purchase agreement, will govern the final configuration and capabilities of the product and we encourage you to review the specification.

Ramp scene at Amsterdam-Schiphol airport in the 1990s. The MD-11 illustrated here, with the name Florence Nightingale, was selected by KLM for the last three excursion flights carrying MD-11 enthusiasts before it was flown to an American aircraft boneyard and stripped of all recyclable parts. *Author's archive*

MD-11 Combi

TECHNOLOGY FOR THE 21ST CENTURY

MCDONNELL DOUGLAS

MD-11 Convertible Freighter

TECHNOLOGY FOR THE 21ST CENTURY

MCDONNELL DOUGLAS

LSAS, these also took place in the background, without a perceptible movement of the control column in the cockpit. Another feature of the MD-11 was a fuel trim tank integrated into the horizontal tail, which, when needed, shifted the aircraft's center of gravity toward the tail, which in cruising flight positively affected the aircraft's angle of attack to the benefit of lowest possible fuel consumption. When the MD-11 is being landed, it must be flown exactly as specified in the handbook, avoiding an excessive sink rate and any control input during touchdown that deviates from the handbook. This is confirmed by landing accidents involving MD-11Fs of the express freight company FedEx on July 31, 1997, at Newark International Airport, and on March 23, 2009, at the Tokyo-Narita airport, as well as the total loss of an MD-11F of Lufthansa Cargo on July 27, 2010, at Riyadh, Saudi Arabia.

Although it has been used exclusively as a freighter since the year 2014, in the beginning the MD-11 was operated as a passenger aircraft by numerous airlines. It is often forgotten that the list of MD-11 customers included such prominent companies as Alitalia, American Airlines, China Airlines, China Eastern, Delta Air Lines, EVA Air, Finnair, Garuda Indonesia, KLM, Korean Airlines, LTU, Swissair, Thai International, VARIG, and VASP—just to mention the best-known airlines. They all flew MD-11s, usually in a comfortable three-class layout with approximately 240 passengers in first, business, and economy classes. A look back at the year 1988 published by Boeing illustrates the MD-11's importance in passenger and freight traffic at that time. The 174 aircraft delivered by January of that year were used on scheduled services by twenty airlines, encompassing 100 destinations in fifty-five countries, with over 270 scheduled flights daily. Since December 1990, the global MD-11 fleet had flown more than 2.7 million flying hours and covered 2 billion kilometers, carrying about seventy million passengers aboard the trijet.

MD-12: AMAZINGLY SIMILAR TO THE A380

The design department of the McDonnell Douglas Aircraft Company recognized the potential slumbering in the MD-11 and further developed from this type an entire family of aircraft with different models of different size and range. In particular, the MD-11 seemed suited to a lengthened fuselage and extended wings. From these initial considerations, between 1988 and the merger with Boeing, many more concepts—some of them thought through to production readiness—were developed, but they all had one thing in common: they were never realized.

The first concept looked into by McDonnell Douglas was initially designated the MD-12. It was based on a lengthened MD-11 fuselage combined with an improved wing, which the Americans had gladly adopted from the Airbus A330/340 program.

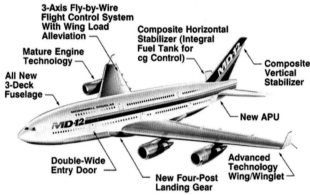

*C*onfiguration Features - MD-12

At first glance the planned MD-12 differed externally very little from the Airbus A380, which was in fact built. *Author's archive*

Together with the MD-XX Long Range, the MD-XX STRETCH was the last thwarted attempt by McDonnell Douglas to offer a stretched version of the MD-11, with even more-fuel-efficient engines, a tail section made of composite materials, and a newly developed, aerodynamically refined wing prior to its merger with Boeing. *Author's archive*

Even after the merger of McDonnell Douglas and Boeing, the MD-11 was initially continued as a Boeing type, before the delivery of the last of 200 aircraft produced marked the end of the MD-11 program in February 2001. *Author's archive*

Probably speculating that Airbus's own plans for long-range aircraft could be put on ice in favor of a partnership in the MD-12 program, in 1988 McDonnell Douglas management made contact with Toulouse. Not surprisingly, the Europeans rejected the advances from California and turned both the A330 and A340 into successes with their own resources.

Douglas refused to become discouraged by this, however, and continued planning for the MD-12 on the basis of the existing but further modified MD-11 wing. For a time a special feature was planned: the building of a panoramic lounge on the lower deck of the MD-12's fuselage, and equipping the aircraft, now called the MD-12X, with two passenger decks. The larger the design on the engineers' drawing boards became, the more obvious became the necessity of designing a completely new wing for the aircraft, which by then had grown to 238 feet in length. In November 1991, McDonnell Douglas and Taiwan Aerospace signed a memorandum of understanding for the joint development and production of the MD-12X, which, starting on December 25, 1991, was officially offered to the airlines. The partners hoped that with sufficient orders a first flight could be made in 1995, followed by the first deliveries to customers two years later. McDonnell Douglas was to have a 51 percent share in the American-Taiwanese joint venture, and Taiwan Aerospace 40 percent. The remaining 9 percent was to go to Asian partners based in Japan and South Korea. It was envisaged not only that the joint venture would be entrusted with the MD-12 program, but that the entire civil aircraft branch of McDonnell Douglas would be transferred to the company, which was jokingly referred to as Asiatic Airbus in the airline industry. But neither this plan nor the joint venture took off.

The three-engined MD-12, with its maximum seating capacity of 520, was offered as an alternative to the four-engined Boeing 747-400 and was to be powered by Rolls-Royce Trent 775 turbofan engines as standard power plants. In January 1992, on the basis of

comments about the MD-12 program received from the airlines, McDonnell Douglas decided to end its development in favor of a four-engined jet, with which its two passenger decks resembled the present-day Airbus A380. The MD-12, which was 208 feet long and designed to carry up to 551 passengers—160 of them on the upper deck alone—over a distance of 9,196 miles, was first presented to the public in April 1992. Once again Taiwan Aerospace was supposed to play a role in this mammoth project, but despite all the sales efforts, no airline warmed to this project, which subsequently disappeared into the desk drawers of the design department.

MD-XX: THE FINAL ATTEMPT

After the failure of its four-engined megaliner project, at first it was again "back to the future" for McDonnell Douglas, which in the 1990s culminated in two types, the MD-XX STRETCH and the MD-XX Long Range. These 100 percent McDonnell Douglas developments based on the MD-11 were in principle a return to the original MD-12 concept of 1998, supplemented by a completely newly developed wing. At the beginning of 1996, it was shown for the first time to a small group of eleven airlines, which intensively took part in the conception of the new family of aircraft. With the newly developed wing with its greater span and increased sweep, the MD-DC-10 was supposed to achieve a performance improvement comparable to the MD-11. In May 1996, McDonnell Douglas president Harry Stonecipher invited representatives of sixty airlines to a conference in Long Beach, at which details of the MD-DC-10 program were presented to the public for the first time. The official program start was planned for December 1996, and the end of the technical-definition phase for October 1997. The final assembly of the two MD-XX versions was to take place at the MD-11 production line in Long Beach.

The concept of the MD-XX STRETCH envisaged stretching the aircraft by 31 feet compared to the MD-11. Thus modified, it would have been capable of carrying 360 passengers in a comfortable three-class seating arrangement over a distance of about 6,835 miles. To avoid exceeding ramp and runway weight limits, it was planned to distribute the maximum takeoff weight of 401 tons over the six wheels of each outer main undercarriage unit and the four wheels of the center main undercarriage unit and the two tires of the nosewheel. The cruising speed of the MD-XX STRETCH was Mach 0.85 for both the passenger and planned freight versions. To ensure an identical type rating for MD-11 and MD-XX pilots, McDonnell Douglas planned to adopt the earlier type's flight deck unchanged for the stretched jet. The tail of the MD-XX STRETCH was, however, a new design that was to be made primarily of composite materials. "Back to the future" was also the motto in the case of the winglets on the wingtips of the MD-XX, which reduced drag and thus fuel consumption. Boeing recalled their design when they designed the winglets for its latest MAX series of its 737 bestseller, which were so similar to those of the MD-XX that they could barely be told apart.

In addition to transporting passengers, McDonnell Douglas also saw great potential in its MD-XX STRETCH as a freighter. With thirty-two standard pallets on the main deck and a further thirteen pallets in the underfloor area, it would even have surpassed the Boeing 777F, with its twenty-seven positions on the main deck and ten positions on the lower deck. But neither the MD-XX STRETCH nor the MD-XX Long Range entered production. This ultra-long-range machine was supposed to have a maximum range of 8,699 miles with 301 passengers onboard. It was planned with the identical maximum takeoff weight as its larger sister, which the shorter MD-XX Long Range achieved by carrying extra fuel for long-range flights. It was also fitted with the modified main undercarriage of the MD-XX STRETCH. Like it, the Long Range had also been conceived as a freighter for the transport of a maximum of twenty-six pallets on the upper deck and nine on the lower deck.

But as optimistic as the McDonnell Douglas managers still were in the first half of 1996, toward the end of the year the manufacturer was forced to realize that the MD-XX would have stretched it financially. Like all previous efforts, this final attempt to bring a new civil development to the market before the merger with Boeing also failed.

MILESTONES OF THE MD-11 PROGRAM

July 29, 1985
The McDonnell Douglas supervisory board authorizes the board to accept orders for the MD-11.

December 30, 1986
Official program start

March 1987
Production of the first components begins.

March 9, 1988
Construction of the first fuselage sections begins in Long Beach.

September 1989
Rollout of the first prototype

January 10, 1990
The first prototype with the registration N111MD makes its first takeoff.

March 1, 1990

First flight by the second MD-11, with the registration N211MD

April 26, 1990

Prototype number 3, with the registration N311MD, is the first aircraft equipped with Pratt & Whitney PW 4460 engines.

August 1, 1990

The fourth MD-11, with the registration N411MD, completes the then-longest flight by a trijet commercial aircraft. The aircraft flew from Anchorage, Alaska, to the McDonnell Douglas test center in Yuma, Arizona, and back in sixteen hours and thirty-five minutes.

November 8, 1990

The American regulatory authority FAA issues the MD-11 its type certification as part of the DC-10 program.

November 29, 1990

In a handover ceremony, the first production aircraft is handed over to Finnair, the type's first customer, at Long Beach.

December 19, 1990

Certification of the MD-11, equipped with Pratt & Whitney PW 4460 engines

April 26, 1991

The MD-11 is certified for category 3B weather minima.

June 6, 1991

The first MD-11G is delivered to Federal Express.

November 6, 1991

The MD-11 is the first aircraft type certified by the newly created European regulatory authority JAA, a predecessor of the present-day EASA, in its thirty-four European member states.

1997

Boeing takes over McDonnell Douglas and continues the MD-11 only in the freight version.

September 2, 1998

Blackest day in the history of the MD-11

Approximately an hour after taking off from John F. Kennedy Airport in New York, Swissair flight SR 111 catches fire on its way to Geneva and crashes into the sea off the coast of Nova Scotia, Canada. All 215 passengers and fourteen crew onboard lost their lives. In the course of the accident investigation by international accident investigators led by the Canadian TSB, a short circuit is discovered in a power cable above the cockpit, whose electric arc caused a fire in the Mylar insulating material in the cockpit. The fire spread quickly between the instrument panels and the external skin above the pilots' heads, and within a few minutes it destroyed important data lines, made the aircraft uncontrollable, and led to its crash. Prior to the SR 111 accident, Mylar was regarded as a fire-retardant material and was installed in the passenger cabins of most Western commercial aircraft as sound and climate insulation. As a consequence of the catastrophe, the use of Mylar was forbidden in aircraft.

February 22, 2011

Lufthansa Cargo receives the last of 200 MD-11s built.

October 26, 2014

KLM makes the last commercial passenger flight by an MD-111.

November 11, 2014

After special flights for aviation enthusiasts, the MD-11 painted in a special finish recalling the close eighty-year link between KLM and Douglas is finally retired.

CHAPTER 11
THE DC-10 IN THE LUFTHANSA GROUP
SELECTION BY THE ATLAS CONSORTIUM

At a meeting on September 23, 1970, the Lufthansa supervisory board authorized the order of four examples of the long-range DC-10-30. This decision had been preceded by an intensive decision process described below, in the course of which the advantages and disadvantages of the Lockheed L-1011 were weighed against those of the DC-10, which was ultimately ordered. Altogether the board ordered eleven aircraft, which were operated by Lufthansa and its charter subsidiary Condor.

In 1969, Lufthansa was searching for a long-range type with the internal designation of Type Y, whose capacity would lie between the Boeing 707-330B and the 747-130. Lufthansa anticipated that the earliest the type could enter service would be 1974. On paper, both the McDonnell Douglas DC-10 and the Lockheed L-1011 fulfilled Lufthansa management's expectations. The German airline discussed which of the two trijets to procure, not only within its

The selection and technical specification of the Lufthansa DC-10-30 took place within the ATLAS consortium. *Lufthansa*

The crane has graced the tails of Lufthansa aircraft since 1955, including those of Douglas Commercial types DC-3, DC-4, DC-8, and DC-10. *Lufthansa*

internal circle of experts but also with its European partners of the ATLAS consortium. The group was originally formed in spring 1968 as a community of purpose for the small Boeing 747 fleets of Air France, Alitalia, Lufthansa, and Sabena and, in 1972, was expanded to include the Spanish airline Iberia. For example, in 1970, Lufthansa began operating three Boeing 747-130s. Operating them single-handedly would have been at least expensive, if not uneconomical. But operating within a community, and with divided roles for the overhauling of airframes, systems, and engines, it was possible to reduce costs to an acceptable level for all the ATLAS partners. As of 1969, Air France assumed responsibility for the major overhaul (D check) of the few jumbo jets of its partners, Lufthansa was named the overhaul center for the 747 power plants, and Alitalia and Sabena became responsible for the overhaul of 747 components. Lufthansa was also responsible for operation of a 747 flight simulator for training of its own pilots and those of the ATLAS partners. In the course of its existence, the cooperative effort for the Boeing 747 Classic was expanded to include other aircraft types: the Boeing 747-200, -300, and -400; Airbus A300, A310, and A340; and the McDonnell Douglas DC-10. However the pan-European community of purpose did not just organize technical support for individual types, it also defined common technical standards for new aircraft types to be procured, and agreed on them contractually with the manufacturers. During the ATLAS group's selection process for a future wide-body trijet, a head-to-head competition developed between Lockheed and Douglas. What Prof. Ernst Simon, who at that time was responsible for the selection of future aircraft types by Lufthansa, thought about the two types is described in the next chapter.

Lufthansa decided in favor of the DC-10-30 because at the end of the 1960s, it was seeking a long-range aircraft whose capacity lay between the Boeing 747-200 and the Boeing 707-330B. *Lufthansa*

In concert with its ATLAS partners, Lufthansa developed extensive technical and commercial studies, which "were supported by a Sabena computer program," as a contemporaneous report states. This was noteworthy from the perspective of the time, since the use of computers in the late 1960s was an absolute exception. Computing did not enter the aviation field on a large scale until the 1970s, slowly replacing the age of the slide rule. In its tough competition battle with Lockheed, it was not until after Douglas made both technical and price concessions to the ATLAS selection committee that the DC-10 and L-1011 were found roughly equal in its estimation. Lufthansa historical documents reveal that it was not technical/ operational differences that tipped the scales in the DC-10's favor; rather, it was financial questions. In the end the L-1011-84-A TriStar long-range version existed only on paper, since both the aircraft maker and its power plant supplier had fallen into financial difficulties, which in the case of Rolls-Royce even resulted in a period of insolvency. As well, the number of firm orders promised by the ATLAS members was not sufficient for Lockheed to launch the long-range version of the TriStar. Another plus in the view of the ATLAS Group was the initial order on June 7, 1969, for fourteen DC-10-30s by the KSSU alliance of KLM, SAS, Swissair, and UTA, which was comparable to ATLAS, whereupon Douglas guaranteed the production start of that model.

As the top body in the group, in autumn 1969 the ATLAS Management Committee directed the so-called ad hoc team to develop a joint specification both for the L-1011 and the DC-10. It would contain a detailed performance and construction description of the aircraft by the airlines; for example, covering cockpit and cabin equipment. For Lufthansa this was the first aircraft procurement

TOP If Lockheed had been able to produce the 84-A long-range version of its L-1011, which it offered to Lufthansa in 1969, the order for the DC-10-30 might never have happened. *Lufthansa*

BOTTOM The copilot carries out the preflight check of a Lufthansa DC-10-30. *Lufthansa*

program in its history in which these responsibilities were not 100 percent assigned to its own technical department but instead were issued to a European group. The objectives of the ten teams employed by ATLAS were to examine the general flight characteristics, noise generation, cockpit layout, electrical systems, structure, equipment in the passenger cabin and cargo hold, engines, hydraulics and pneumatics, and control systems of the two wide-body jets, and to completely standardize them for the ATLAS partners. The only differences between the aircraft would be the colors of their cabins and their external airline liveries. Another ATLAS ad hoc team led by Lufthansa conducted contract negotiations with the manufacturers Lockheed and Douglas as well as the engine makers General Electric (DC-10) and Rolls-Royce (L-1011). The goal of the negotiations, on behalf of all the partners, was to obtain the most-favorable contract conditions, such as price guarantees and advantageous payment terms. In keeping with the motto "Together we are strong," the ATLAS partners threw their combined fleet into the balance during the negotiations—but in the end they ordered their aircraft individually. The final decision as to the purchase of a new aircraft type also remained with the individual ATLAS partners, and there was no pressure in the group to order a jointly defined aircraft type. In the end, Lufthansa, together with Alitalia and Sabena, decided on the DC-10-30 early in 1970, while Air France could not force itself to decide to purchase and instead expanded its Boeing 747 fleet. Despite this, Air France took part in the joint distribution of work within the ATLAS group.

Since all the DC-10-30s ordered by the ATLAS partners were in principle identical, they were able to maintain a joint stock of materials and spare parts, as well as a common engineering body,

This advertisement by McDonnell Douglas also includes the logos of the DC-10 customers in the ATLAS consortium: Alitalia, Lufthansa, and Sabena.
Dave Robinson collection

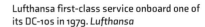
Lufthansa first-class service onboard one of its DC-10s in 1979. *Lufthansa*

and shared maintenance of this aircraft type. On the basis of this cooperation, ATLAS Airlines also operated a common DC-10 flight simulator for the training of its pilots. Looking back, the decision by ATLAS and KSSU for the DC-10-30 was the correct one, since Rolls-Royce failed in its efforts to further develop the RB.211 turbofan, the sole power plant for the L-1011, so that it could provide sufficient thrust for the projected long-range L-1011-84.

The joint specification for the DC-10 within the ATLAS group proceeded so well that the partners expanded their common approach in the next step toward the Airbus A300B project. By July 1971, the ATLAS technicians submitted more than 1,000 "Requests for Change" to the basic Airbus layout of the A300B2 and B4. Most were marginal requirements, some of which concerned only individual formulations in the technical documents, but there remained 300 larger "Master Changes" whose implementation was negotiated between Airbus

management and the ATLAS committee. On October 7, 1971, the ATLAS representatives presented their findings concerning the expected profitability of the A300B on the route networks of the four partner airlines. As well, they had drawn up standard sales contracts for the A300B on the basis of the ATLAS specification for the type. As in the case of the selection of the future wide-body long-range jet, here again ATLAS did not place orders; rather, the participating airlines ordered their first-generation A300Bs in direct negotiations with Airbus.

In the case of the DC-10, maintenance work remained at the individual maintenance bases of the ATLAS partners, as it had done with the Boeing 747. The key to the partnership, however, was the major overhaul of airframes by Alitalia in Rome, of the General Electric engines by Air France in Paris, and of equipment by Sabena

The Lufthansa DC-10 fleet's home airport of Frankfurt/Main was the starting point for its worldwide network of routes. *Lufthansa*

in Brussels, Lufthansa in Hamburg, and Alitalia in Rome. The Italian capital also became the selected location of the DC-10 flight simulator. The division of the work package took into consideration the existing 747 sharing program and the principles laid down in the ATLAS framework contract:

- rationalization through a sensible division of labor
- exploitation of existing capacities
- distribution of work between the partners, corresponding to the volume of work introduced, regardless of fleet size
- no continuous specialization by individual partners on certain work; for example, engine overhaul

Lufthansa in particular had no large role in the overhauling of the DC-10, since it was already responsible for the overhauling of Boeing 747 engines, and Alitalia seemed the best suited of the partners to overhaul the airframes.

Although not involved on a large scale quantitatively, by overhauling certain onboard electronic equipment, Lufthansa had a major qualitative share in the DC-10 program. For this work package, the ERI workshops at the Hamburg technical base—now Lufthansa Technik AG—created the so-called Automatic Test Equipment (ATE) so as to be able to rationally carry out the overhaul of the Performance and Failure Assessment Monitor (PAFAM) and the Air Data Computer for the aircraft of the ATLAS consortium. The PAFAM was for its time a very advanced system, which, by using a color display screen, marked the projected touchdown point on the runway in front of the pilot during the approach to land—and, if necessary, gave a recommendation to break off the approach and go around. The PAFAM did not actively intervene in the control of the DC-10, however. The ATE, procured by Lufthansa at a cost of almost a million deutsch marks, paid off for the company, since it could also be used in the overhaul of equipment in other Lufthansa types: the Boeing 707, 727, and 737.

The ATLAS consortium lasted until 1994, after Lufthansa had retired its last DC-10-30 on December 1 of that year, and the partners agreed that in the future they would technically and operationally maintain their much-larger fleets individually.

The DC-10-30 made its first flight in Lufthansa colors on January 14, 1974, on the route from Frankfurt/Main to Tokyo, and the eleven aircraft delivered by 1977 were seen on the airline's entire route network, as well as three others on the tourist routes operated by its then charter subsidiary Condor. While the big trijet fit into Lufthansa's capacity gap between the 707 and 747, Condor used its three jets delivered from 1979 to replace the two Boeing 747s it had previously operated. In Condor's charter version, 373 passengers could be accommodated in a single-class seating arrangement, while Lufthansa offered its passengers a more comfortable seating configuration with twenty-two seats in first class, sixty-six in business class, and 141 economy seats. After Lufthansa divested itself of its last DC-10-30 in 1994, the Condor jets remained in the airline's fleet for another five years, until 1999.

The holiday airline Condor was part of the Lufthansa Group during the period in which it operated the DC-10-30 between 1979 and 1999. Like the fuselages of the aircraft flown by American Airlines, that of this Condor DC-10 is unpainted, and its natural-metal skin gleams in the sunshine. *Condor*

CHAPTER 12
DC-10 IN THE
LUFTHANSA GROUP
LOCKHEED TRISTAR
WAS THE FAVORITE

In 1969, the office of Professor Ernst Simon received an interesting offer from Burbank, California. From the 1960s to the 1980s, Simon, the director of Lufthansa's Main Department of Technical Projects, who died in 2015, was responsible for the assessment and selection of new aircraft types in Lufthansa's engineering department. At the end of the 1960s, the topic was procurement of a long-range type to close the gap in seating capacity between the Boeing 707-330 and the Boeing 747-130 jumbo jet. The choice was between the Douglas DC-10 and Lockheed L-1011, both of which were in the development stage. In a conversation with the author in 2013, Professor Simon recalled that "My choice fell on the L-1011 TriStar. It was the most technically advanced aircraft and was designed by Kelly Johnson, probably the best designer of his day." It was obvious that the two designs were very similar at first glance, but Simon knew that they differed greatly in detail. "I did not like the arrangement

Lufthansa was about to add its logo to the circle of initial customers for the L-1011, as seen on the fuselage of this L-1011. After completion, the aircraft was first used by Lockheed in its flight test program and for sales tours around the world, before it was delivered to Eastern Air Lines. *Jon Proctor*

Prof. Ernst Simon in 2013 with a drawing of the L-1011 TriStar in Lufthansa colors, given to him by Lockheed. *Author's archive*

The L-1011-84-A long-range version, which was offered to Lufthansa but never built, was to have been capable of flying from Frankfurt to the West Coast of the United States. In 1969, the technical consortium ATLAS—Lufthansa, Sabena, Air France, and Alitalia—prepared a joint specification for the possible purchase of the L-1011. Each of the participating airlines would have ordered the aircraft from Lockheed individually, but they would have been ordered with an identical technical standard to allow simplified maintenance within the consortium. This was an idea that was in fact implemented with the DC-10-30, which was actually purchased, and also for other types used by the ATLAS partners, such as the Airbus A300 and Boeing 747.

There were several reasons why Lufthansa did not purchase the L-1011. One was that Lockheed, which was already having financial difficulties, could not bring itself to produce the L-1011-84-A long-range version. The prospective order size by the ATLAS consortium partners appeared too small to the Lockheed managers to risk a production start based on this order. On the other hand, faced with the financial crises looming over Lockheed and Rolls-Royce, the ATLAS partners hesitated. It was a decision that would be proven correct by Rolls-Royce's insolvency in 1971, and the resulting halt in production of the RB-211 turbofan for more than a year. By then, Lufthansa had already decided in favor of the safer choice, in the form of the competing DC-10-30.

of the DC-10's center engine. Compared to the L-1011 it was mounted much higher and was difficult to access. In design terms this also meant a higher structural weight. The effect of this was that the L-1011 had a better takeoff performance compared to the DC-10. The L-1011's design also included more integrally milled large components, and the horizontal tail was of very advanced design. Not least, compared to the DC-10's CF6-50s, the Rolls-Royce RB 211 three-shaft engines which the L-1011 offered were more technically advanced, quieter, lighter, and also more economical. Overall the L-1011 was an outstanding aircraft, which was used successfully by many airlines from the mid-1970s."

The California airline PSA planned to use five L-1011s on its medium-range routes; however, it accepted just two. The remaining jets went to German airline LTU and were given the registrations D-AERI, D-AERE, and D-AERU. In contrast to the long-range L-1011-84-A version, with a range of about 6,835 miles, the model actually built by Lockheed at the beginning of the 1970s had a range of just 3,417 miles. Not until the shortened and thus lighter L-1011-500 did the type achieve a range of almost 6,200 miles in the 1980s. *Jon Proctor*

CHAPTER 13
MD-11 IN SERVICE WITH THE LUFTHANSA GROUP
LUFTHANSA CARGO

On September 5, 1996, champagne corks popped at the McDonnell Douglas group stand at the Farnborough Airshow in Britain. The sales team had finally interested Lufthansa Cargo AG, the Lufthansa group's freight subsidiary, in the MD-11, after the airline's passenger division had selected the competing Airbus A340 in January.

The contract signed by Wilhelm Althen, then chairman of the board of Lufthansa Cargo AG, and Edward Bavaria, deputy president of the Douglas Aircraft Company, covered the firm order for five McDonnell Douglas MD-11F cargo aircraft and options for another seven examples of what was then the most technologically advanced trijet. While the salesman Althen, in a businessman-like and sober manner, dryly extolled the MD-11 as "a sensible addition to the all-cargo fleet," Michael M. Sears, president of the Douglas Aircraft Company, found more-flowery words for the signing of the contract: "Lufthansa Cargo's decision to introduce a new aircraft type, the

Impressions of the Lufthansa Cargo MD-11. The trijet was still in use by the Lufthansa freight subsidiary in January 2019 and was gradually being repainted in the new company colors. *Lufthansa Cargo*

I LOOK FORWARD TO EVERY FLIGHT IN OUR MD-11FS. THEY ARE VERY SPECIAL AIRCRAFT. CHARACTERISTIC FEATURES ON THE OUTSIDE; A COMFORTABLE, BRIGHT, AND SPACIOUS WORKPLACE ON THE INSIDE. WITH OUR 'ELEVENS' WE CARRY THE LUFTHANSA CARGO SPIRIT ALL OVER THE WORLD. SUNRISE OVER THE SAHARA, TWILIGHT OVER THE ANDES, THE STARRY SKY ABOVE THE STEPPES: SUCH MOMENTS CAUSE EVERY PILOT'S HEART TO BEAT FASTER.

—Capt. Claus Richter, vice president,

Transport Management & Flight Operations, lead operating manager

Actually the name of a global air freight consortium, WOW is a word that comes from the lips of many MD-11 fans, especially on seeing the elegant lines of the trijet. *Lufthansa Cargo*

In the medium term, comparably large but more efficient, quieter, and more environmentally friendly Boeing 777Fs will completely replace the MD-11 in the Lufthansa Cargo fleet. *Lufthansa Cargo*

MD-11F, to its freighter fleet is confirmation that the MD-11F is a good choice among the world's cargo aircraft. There are only a few airlines in the world whose decisions are watched very closely by others, and Lufthansa is one of them."

At that time the fleet of the Lufthansa freight subsidiary, founded on November 30, 1994, consisted entirely of Boeing 747-200F jumbo jets, after the last of five McDonnell Douglas DC-8-73s had left the Lufthansa cargo fleet on May 8, 1996. Because the remaining 747-200Fs, with a maximum payload of 112 tons, were too large for many of Lufthansa's freight routes, with its cargo load of about 102 tons the MD-11F—deliveries of which were to begin in June 1998—seemed a good addition, and not just from a capacity point of view.

McDonnell Douglas promised a "green aircraft" with 39 percent lower fuel consumption and drastically reduced emission levels compared to the 747-200F: 43 percent less nitric oxide, 99.6 percent fewer hydrocarbons, and 69 percent less carbon dioxide. Also, compared to the Boeing 747-200F the MD-11F was significantly quieter, and unlike the second-generation jumbo jet, it was able to meet the strict limits of the then-lowest noise category. The MD-11F also offered a big advantage in personnel costs thanks to its two-man glass cockpit, obviating the need for the flight engineer still required by the 747-200F.

It is no surprise, therefore, not only that the MD-11F completely replaced the 747-200F in Lufthansa Cargo by 2005, but that the airline's fleet gradually grew to nineteen aircraft. Among them was the last of 200 MD-11s built at Long Beach, registered D-ALCN, which was handed over to Lufthansa Cargo on January 25, 2001.

The last brand-new MD-11F delivered to the "cargo cranes" bore the registration D-ALCM and joined the fleet on February 22 of that year. Five used MD-11Fs, which Boeing converted from passenger machines into freighters before they were handed over to Lufthansa Cargo, followed in 2004 and 2005—they are no longer in service with the airline.

In 2011, the Lufthansa group's supervisory board decided to procure five Boeing 777-200F freighters with a maximum cargo capacity of 113 tons, which were delivered between 2013 and 2015 to supplement and partly replace the airline's fleet of MD-11s. In 2019, another eleven aircraft of this type were in service with AeroLogic, a joint venture by DHL Express and Lufthansa Cargo. While the Boeing jetliners transport express freight on behalf of DHL during the week, they are available to Lufthansa Cargo on the weekends. The delivery of three more 777Fs—two for Lufthansa Cargo and one for AeroLogic—as well as the retirement of two MD-11Fs, also occured in 2019.

While the MD-11 was a quantum leap because of its lower fuel consumption, noise levels, and emission values compared to the Boeing 747-200F, the introduction of the twin-jet Boeing 777-200F represents another drastic improvement in all environmental parameters.

In the winter of 2018–19, Lufthansa Cargo was still flying twelve of its original fleet of nineteen MD-11Fs. One aircraft, with the registration D-ALCQ, was lost in a landing accident at Riyadh in Saudi Arabia on July 27, 2010, and the remaining six retired trijets were sold to other airlines.

CHAPTER 14
LTU'S MD-11S
WORLD PREMIERE
ABOVE THE CLOUDS

Two German tourist airlines, LTU of Dusseldorf and Aero Lloyd based at the Frankfurt airport, selected the MD-11. The latter planned to lease its trijets from the Swiss holding company ADO Finance, which was involved in Aero Lloyd and the Egyptian airline ZAS. ADO Finance ordered three MD-11s from McDonnell Douglas in February 1989 for use by its two investments and also signed up for three more options. But neither Aero Lloyd nor ZAS received even a single MD-11, since they put on hold their international expansion plans even before their planned delivery date.

And so LTU was the only German airline to operate a passenger version of the MD-11. On December 21, 1988, in Long Beach, LTU management signed a purchase agreement for three aircraft with which to expand its long-range tourist business—followed shortly thereafter by exercising one option for a fourth MD-11. The next ceremony, in Toulouse, France, followed one day after the contract

One of four red-and-white MD-11s operated by LTU on its tourist network of routes between 1991 and 1998, which together with the Airbus A330-300 replaced the L-1011 in LTU service. *LTU*

was signed in California. There LTU placed an order for Airbus A330s for its midrange-route network to the warm-water destinations around the Mediterranean. When the first MD-11 entered service with LTU's line and charter service, its subsidiary companies LTE and LTU-South were already flying Boeing 757s and 767s, followed in 1995 by the first A330-300s. The Dusseldorf airline did not bid farewell to its cherished Lockheed TriStars—with which LTU had grown in size and importance in the German air charter market in the 1970s—until 1996.

The first MD-11 finished in LTU's legendary red-and-white colors arrived in Dusseldorf from Long Beach on December 20, 1999, and just a few days later it achieved fame throughout the country. During a live broadcast by ARD Television on New Year's Eve 1991–92, pianist Julius Frantz and fifty-three members of a symphony orchestra gave a twenty-minute concert above the clouds. So that the images would be transmitted to the ground clearly and then broadcast to television sets in the Federal Republic, the LTU jet circled at an altitude of 22,965 feet over a radar-equipped armored vehicle of the Bundeswehr, which transmitted the signals it received from the air to a television transmission truck, which in turn sent the moving images by satellite to a broadcasting center, from where they reached millions of homes via satellite dishes, cable, or radio transmission.

The world's largest three-engined passenger jet entered regular service with LTU at the beginning of 1992. The MD-11 was also used on connecting flights to North America after LTU received approval from the German Ministry of Transport on May 1, 1990. The red-and-white MD-11s were also seen at South and Central American airports such as Rio de Janeiro and Acapulco, however. But after just a few years, LTU management was forced to realize that its fleet mix was too diversified, and that a small airline such as LTU could not afford four different aircraft types in its small fleet of about twenty jets. The decision was therefore made to initially concentrate flying activities on the Airbus A330 and A321/A320. As a result of this strategy, all four MD-11s left the LTU fleet in November 1998 and were given to Swissair, which at that time was owned by the Swiss holding company SAir Group, as was LTU. They operated successfully there until the airline's insolvency and the resulting grounding of Swissair in October 2001.

LTU, however, succeeded in staying in the air for another six years in difficult times—especially after the attacks of September 11, 2001—with new owners. Buried under a mountain of debt—200 million Euros—in 2007 it was forced to place itself under the protecting wings of Air Berlin, by which it was completely taken over a short time later.

CHAPTER 15
THE DC-10S OF KLM, SAS, SWISSAIR, AND UTA
SELECTION BY THE KSSU CONSORTIUM

The members of the KSSU alliance among KLM, SAS, Swissair, and UTA fired the starting shot for development of the long-range DC-10-30 by placing an initial order for fourteen aircraft plus twenty-two options on June 7, 1969.

Decades before the alliances in air transport, which are quite common today, Swissair and SAS carried out the selection, definition, and technical maintenance of their aircraft jointly. In 1958, the two airlines began their cooperation, with seven DC-8-32 long-range jets ordered by SAS and three by Swissair, which except for their cabin colors and external livery were identical. When both airlines ordered both SE 210 Caravelles and Convair CV 990 Coronados, their partnership was extended to include these two types. Swissair dedicated itself to maintaining the CV 990, while SAS carried out general overhauls on the DC-8s and Caravelles of both airlines, The

Dutch airline KLM had been an informal partner in the alliance since 1963, when it initially began looking after the JT3 power plants of the DC-8-32s of all three airlines. In 1967, it officially became the third partner in the consortium, which was expanded by the technical work package for the Douglas DC-9, which KLM, SAS, and Swissair all had ordered.

When the jumbo age dawned toward the end of the 1960s, SAS, Swissair, and KLM—like the partners of the ATLAS consortium described in the previous chapter—also faced the challenge of having to operate and maintain a total of fifteen examples of the Boeing 747 in a way that made good fiscal sense. This led in 1968 to the signing of the KSS (KLM-SAS-Swissair) agreement, which defined common technical and operational standards for this type and set down a division of tasks for its overhaul. SAS took over overhauling of the Pratt & Whitney JT9D engines at its Linta workshops in

The first SAS DC-10 in the paint hangar prior to its delivery to the Scandinavian airline in 1974. SAS

Stockholm, while KLM carried out D checks on the partners' aircraft at Amsterdam. The APUs (auxiliary power units) of the 747 fleets were looked after by the French UTA, after it had expanded the consortium of three by joining in February 1970, resulting in the KSSU quartet. A flight simulator operated by KLM at Amsterdam was used to train KSSU 747 pilots.

The KSSU organization, initially formed for ten years, was headed by an eight-man management committee, comprising two top managers from each airline. Other work groups concerned themselves with the organization of KSSU cooperation, such as setting computing standards and legal as well as financial details. The definition of technical standards and the selection of new aircraft types were, however, the responsibility of the Long Term Advisory Group. After

the Lockheed L-1011-84-A had also been rejected, KLM, SAS, and Swissair agreed on the definition of the McDonnell Douglas DC-10, launching the DC-10-30 long-range version with an order for fourteen aircraft plus twenty-two options on June 7, 1969. A minor but noticeable detail compared to the DC-10s of the ATLAS consortium was the different engine instruments in the cockpit. While ATLAS gave preference to round instruments, KSSU chose vertical-scale indicators for displaying engine values. In addition to the technical systems, common standards were laid down for the cabin design in particular, which apart from different colors of fabrics and cabin equipment did not differ from one another.

Analogous to Lufthansa in the ATLAS consortium, in the KSSU alliance SAS also gave the largest work packages to its partners,

SAS maintained a "skybar" for its first-class guests onboard its DC-10s, with a wide selection of alcoholic beverages. *SAS*

Swissair was responsible for the overhauling of the aircraft structure, not only for its own DC-10 fleet but also for those of the KSSU partners.
ETH-Bibliothek Zurich, Swissair

The DC-10 also looked elegant in the Swissair look of the 1980s. *ETH-Bibliothek Zurich, Swissair*

Arrival of the last scheduled passenger flight by an MD-11 on October 26, 2014. This ended not just a chapter in the McDonnell Douglas story but also an eighty-year-old tradition by KLM, whose first Douglas DC-2 entered service eight decades before. *KLM*

since it had already taken on the extensive task of overhauling the engines of the combined 747 fleets. KLM in Amsterdam was responsible for overhauling the CF6-50 engines of the KSSU DC-10s; Swissair, for airframe overhauls in Zurich; and UTA, for technical maintenance of the undercarriages and APUs mounted in the tail as autonomous power supplies. As a special feature, in addition to its own five DC-10-30s, SAS brought its subsidiary Thai Airways International, with a fleet of two aircraft, into the consortium. This partnership was extended to include Thai Airways' Airbus A300B4s in 1978. While SAS carried out D checks (heavy maintenance checks) at Stockholm-Arlanda, their General Electric CF6-50 engines were overhauled by KLM in Amsterdam, and their APUs in Paris.

EIGHTY YEARS OF DOUGLAS TRADITION

With KLM, SAS, and Swissair, three of the most loyal customers of the Douglas Commercial DC series were combined in the KSSU alliance. Together, these three airlines had operated every commercial aircraft produced by Douglas and McDonnell Douglas with the exception of the DC-1: beginning with the DC-2 of 1934, to the MD-95, the last passenger jet produced in Long Beach before MDC was bought by Boeing in 1997. The last MD-95 (Boeing 717) of SAS's Finnish subsidiary Blue 1 did not leave the fleet until October 2015, when the trio's last Douglas jet was retired.

Employees of the Dutch airline KLM had a particularly emotional moment a year earlier, when on November 11, 2014, three flights on an MD-11 that was retired the same day were organized for aviation enthusiasts, marking the end of the eighty-year partnership between Douglas and KLM. The liaison between the Douglas Aircraft Company and KLM began in 1934 with the twin-engined DC-2 and even included the DC-5, which was purchased by no other airline. The KLM DC-2 with the name Uiver became a legend, competing in the category for commercial aircraft in the MacRobertson air race from England to Australia in 1934.

KLM had already carried out the last scheduled flight by an MD-11 on October 26, 2014: flight KL 672 from Montreal, Canada, to Amsterdam. On the occasion of this memorable moment, the elegant McDonnell Douglas jet was given an honorary shower by the airport firefighting vehicles on its way to the terminal. KLM honored the end of its decades-long partnership with the special marking KLM–Douglas Aviation History, and a listing on the fuselage of all the Douglas commercial aircraft flown by the airline. The then-twenty-one-year-old aircraft, dubbed Audrey Hepburn, not only was the last trijet used by KLM; it also marked the MD-11's finale as a passenger jet. Since that day, the type has flown exclusively as the MD-11F cargo version. And what happened to "Audrey Hepburn" after the last guests had left its farewell party in the KLM hangar? Just a week later, it was flown from Amsterdam to the aircraft boneyard at the Mojave Air & Space Port in the California desert, where it has since slowly been stripped of all usable parts. Hardly a worthy end for a jet with such a notable history.

THE DOUGLAS AIRCRAFT FAMILY IN SERVICE WITH KLM, SAS, AND SWISSAIR

	DC-1	DC-2	DC-3	DC-4	DC-5	DC-6	DC-7	DC-8	DC-9	DC-10	MD-80	MD-11	MD-90-30	MD-95*
KLM	-	x	x	x	x	x	x	x	x	x		x		
SAS	-		x	x		x	x	x	x	x	x		x	x
Swissair	-	x	x	x		x	x	x	x	x	x			

*SAS subsidiaries Blue 1 and Spanair

The KLM house colors blue and white adorned all commercial airliners purchased from Douglas and McDonnell Douglas under the Douglas Commercial brand name—and the Dutch airline's MD-11s. *KLM*

CHAPTER 16
SPECIFICATIONS
DC-10/MD-11/MD-XX

The following are basic specifications of the McDonnell Douglas DC-10 family, as well as of the various MD-11 variants.

The MD-XX STRETCH, whose design was strongly based on the DC-10, was never built. It was to have had a longer fuselage, wings with a greater span, and a tail section made of composite materials. With its passenger capacity of between 300 and 400 seats, it would have been a competitor for the Airbus A-340-300 and the Boeing 747-400 and 777-300 models. The three planned MD-XX variants are described in detail here, since their development had progressed to the production-ready stage and was halted only by MDC's financial woes, which ultimately led to the takeover of McDonnell Douglas by Boeing in 1997. After the merger of the two organizations, Boeing canceled development of the MD-XX in favor of its own 747 and 777.

DC-10-10	
First flight	August 29, 1970
Delivery to first customers American and United on July 29, 1971	
Wingspan	153 ft.
Length	182 ft.
Height	58 ft.
Power plants	3 x General Electric GE CF6-6D, each producing 40,000 lbs. maximum takeoff thrust
Alternative power plants for the DC-10-15 version:	3 x General Electric GE CF6-50C2-F
Maximum takeoff thrust	46,500 pounds
Cruise speed	600 mph
Range	4,400 mi.
Passenger capacity	255–380

Source: McDonnell Douglas

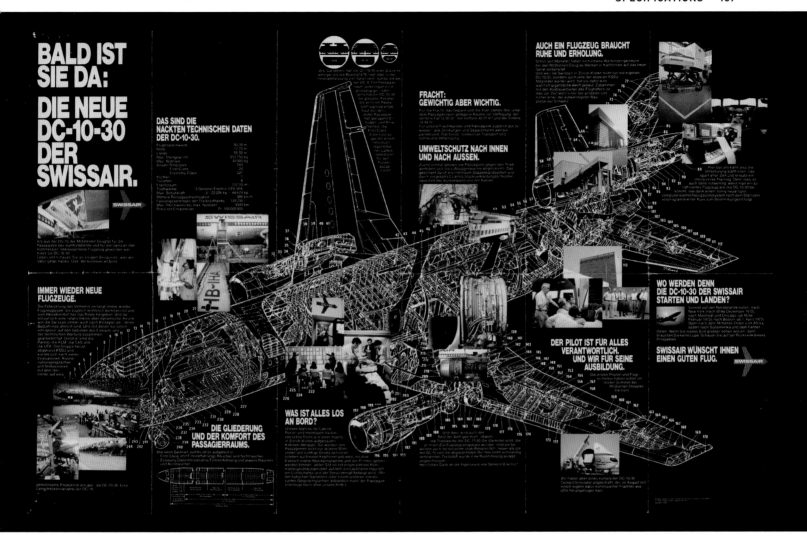

This brochure containing technical details of its then-new DC-10 was published by Swissair in 1974. *Author's archive*

DC-10-30

First flight	June 21, 1972
Delivery to first customers Swissair and KLM on November 21, 1972	
Wingspan	165.3 ft.
Tailplane span	71.2 ft.
Fin height	58 ft.
Top of fuselage height	28 ft.
Overall length / fuselage length	181 ft. / 170 ft.
Fuselage width	19.7 ft.
Main undercarriage track width	35 ft.
Distance between ground and engines	#1 & #3: 2.95 ft.
Distance between ground and wingtips	14.8 ft.
Maximum taxi weight	279 tons
Maximum takeoff weight	277 tons
Maximum landing weight	201.5 tons
Maximum weight without fuel	184 tons
Maximum payload	47.5 tons
Maximum fuel capacity	36,560 gal.
Maximum available fuel, including lines and engines	36,651 gal.
Maximum cruise speed	546.8 mph
Maximum range with maximum payload	4,810 mi.
Maximum range	7,135 mi.
Power plants	3 x General Electric CF6-50C2
Maximum takeoff thrust	52,000 pounds
Cruise speed	600 mph
Minimum takeoff runway length	9,600 ft. (59°F) 12,749 ft. (88°F at elevation of 2,000 ft.)

Source: Brochure, Aircraft for Sale, McDonnell Douglas DC-10-30 (Lufthansa)

DC-10-40

First flight	February 28, 1972
Delivery to first customer Northwest Orient on November 10, 1972	
Wingspan	165 ft.
Length	182 ft.
Height	58 ft.
Power plants	3 x Pratt & Whitney JT9D-20W, each producing 49,400 lbs. maximum takeoff thrust
Alternative power plants	3 x Pratt & Whitney JT9D-59A, each producing 53,000 lbs. maximum takeoff thrust
Cruise speed	600 mph
Range	5,350–6,500 mi.
Passenger capacity	255–380

Source: McDonnell Douglas

DC-10-30CF

First flight	February 28, 1973
Delivery to first customers Overseas Nation and Trans International on April 17, 1973	
Wingspan	165 ft.
Length	181.7 ft.
Height	58 ft.
Power plants	3 x Pratt & Whitney JT9D-20W, each producing 49,400 lbs. maximum takeoff thrust
Alternative power plants	3 x Pratt & Whitney JT9D-59A, each producing 53,000 lbs. maximum takeoff thrust
Cruise speed	600 mph
Range	5,350–6,500 mi.
Passenger capacity	255–380

Source: McDonnell Douglas

Like its partner airlines KLM and SAS, Swissair was also a loyal Douglas customer. Beginning with the DC-2 in 1934, it ordered a total of nine types from the Douglas Commercial series, as well as the MD-11. *ETH-Bibliothek Zurich, Swissair*

The MD-XX Long Range was one of the last two hopes of the McDonnell Douglas Aircraft Company before it was absorbed by Boeing in 1997. Neither this developed version of the MD-11 with extremely long range nor its sister model the MD-XX STRETCH were built. *Author's archive*

The MD-11Fs of the Lufthansa freight subsidiary also look very elegant in the latest Lufthansa paint scheme. *Lufthansa Cargo*

MD-11

First flight	January 10, 1990
Wingspan	170 ft.
Length	200.8 ft.
Height	57.7 ft.
Wing area	3,649 ft.^{2}
Wing sweep	35 degrees
Cabin width	18.3 ft.
Fuel capacity	38,727 gal.
Maximum takeoff weight	312.7 tons
Maximum range	6,524 mi.
Cruise speed	553 mph
Power plants	3 x Pratt & Whitney PW4460
Maximum takeoff thrust	60,000 lbs.
Passenger capacity	408

Information for the MD-11 passenger version for LTU
Source: LTU

Additional Information for the MD-11F Fleet of Lufthansa Air Cargo

MAIN DECK	
26 positions	8 x 10.4 ft.
Side cargo door (H x W)	8.4 x 11.7 ft.
LOWER DECK	
Forward cargo hold	six positions: maximum 8 x 10.4 ft.
Forward cargo hold door	5.5 x 8.7 ft.
Aft cargo hold: four positions maximum 5.5 x 8.7 ft. or 14 LD3 containers	
Aft cargo hold door	5.5 x 8.7 ft.
Cargo hold 5	unsecured loads only
Bulk cargo hold door	3 x 2.5 ft.
LOADING HEIGHT	
Main deck	maximum 8 ft.
Lower deck	maximum 5.3 ft.
Standard load capacity	205,536 lbs.

MD-11 Freighter

Wingspan	170 ft.
Length	200.8 ft.
Height	57.7 ft.
Wing area	3,649 ft.^{2}
Wing sweep	35 degrees
Cargo compartment width	18.3 ft.
Fuel capacity	258,721 lbs.
Maximum takeoff weight	312.7 tons
Maximum weight without fuel	225.6 tons
Empty weight	148 tons
Maximum freight volume	21,287 ft.^{3}
Maximum payload	97 tons
Maximum range with 97-ton payload	3,728 mi.
Power plants	3 x Pratt & Whitney PW4462

Information for the MD-11F for World Airways
Source: McDonnell Douglas

MD-11 Convertible Freighter

Wingspan	170 ft.
Length	200.8 ft.
Height	57.7 ft.
Wing area	3,649 ft.^{2}
Wing sweep	35 degrees
Cargo compartment width	18.3 ft.
Fuel capacity	258,721 lbs.
Maximum takeoff weight	312.7 tons
Maximum landing weight	236 tons
Maximum weight without fuel	225.6 tons
Empty weight	148 tons (passenger configuration) 132 tons (freighter configuration)
Maximum freight volumes	5,163 ft.^{3} (passenger configuration) 19,670 ft.^{3} (freighter configuration)
Maximum payload	97 tons
Maximum range (passenger version)	5,857 mi. with 56-ton maximum payload
Maximum range freight version	4,722 mi. with 83.5-ton maximum payload
Power plants	3 x Pratt & Whitney PW4462

Information for the MD-11 Convertible Freighter for World Airways
Source: McDonnell Douglas

MD-11 Combi

Length	201 ft.
Height	57.7 ft.
Wing area	3,649 ft.²
Wing sweep	35 degrees
Cargo hold width	18.3 ft.
Fuel capacity	258,721 lbs.
Maximum takeoff weight	315 tons
Maximum landing weight	240.7 tons
Maximum weight without fuel	225 tons
Empty weight	143 tons
Maximum payload	55 tons
Maximum range passenger version	5,857 mi. with 51-ton maximum payload
Maximum range	6,490 mi.
Power plants	3 x Pratt & Whitney PW4460
Alternate power plants	General Electric CF6-80C2

Source: McDonnell Douglas

MD-XX STRETCH

Wingspan	213 ft.
Length	232 ft.
Cargo hold width	18.3 ft.
Maximum takeoff weight	401 tons
Maximum landing weight	284 tons
Empty weight	190 tons
Maximum payload	55 tons
Fuel capacity	54,419 gal.
Maximum range	6,984 mi.
Maximum altitude	35,105 ft.
Cruise speed	Mach 0.85
Freight capacity	32 pallets on the main deck 13 pallets on the lower deck

All information for planned freight version.
Source: McDonnell Douglas

MD-XX STRETCH

Wingspan	213 ft.
Length	232 ft.
Cargo hold width	18.3 ft.
Maximum takeoff weight	401 tons
Maximum landing weight	284 tons
Empty weight	190 tons
Maximum payload	55 tons
Fuel capacity	54,419 gal.
Maximum range	6,984 mi.
Maximum altitude	35,105 ft.
Cruise speed	Mach 0.85
Passenger capacity (three classes)	360 seats

All information for planned passenger version
Source: McDonnell Douglas

MD-XX Long Ranch

Length	200.8 ft.
Wingspan	213 ft.
Cabin width	18.3 ft.
Maximum takeoff weight	401 tons
Maximum landing weight	254 tons
Empty weight	177 tons
Maximum payload	107 tons
Fuel capacity	79,251 gal.
Maximum range	8,930 mi. with passengers and freight 9,965 mi. with 301 passengers no freight
Passengers capacity (three classes)	301 seats
As freighter	26 pallets on the main deck 9 pallets on the lower deck
Maximum altitude	35,105 ft.
Cruise speed	Mach 0.85

Source: McDonnell Douglas

THE AUTHOR
WOLFGANG BORGMANN

Wolfgang Borgmann's enthusiasm for aviation was passed on to him by his parents, who were active in the aviation field. In his early years he began building up an aviation historical collection that provides numerous rare photos and documents, as well as exciting background information for his books. Since April 2000, Borgmann has been active as an author and freelance aviation journalist.